BEAUTIFUL & BELIEVABLE

THE REASON FOR MY HOPE.

By Clarke Dixon

ISBN: 9798836457112

This book has been written with much gratitude to my Aunt Marabeth who took on the tedious task of proofreading the original draft. Her Northern Irish grammar may be a wee bit different than my Canadian! Any errors are mine.

While I have tried to do the right thing and give citations where possible, much of what I learned, I cannot tell you when and where I first learned it. My purpose is simply to take the profound and sometimes ponderous writing of experts, and make it short and sweet. I would be overjoyed if this short book led you to the experts, perhaps to the works listed in the bibliography which have shaped my understanding.

Clarke Dixon
clarkedixon@me.com
P.O.Box 837
Colborne, ON K0K 1S0
www.clarkedixon.wordpress.com

To my sons, Skylar, Hunter, and Aidan.

Introduction   1

Part One: Is Christianity Beautiful?

A Beautiful View of Science?   4

A Beautiful Vision For Thought?   11

A Beautiful Vision For Religion?   15

A Beautiful Vision For A Relationship with God?   20

A Beautiful Vision For Our Relationship with Others?   26

A Beautiful Vision of God?   31

A beautiful Engagement with Non-Christians?   37

A Beautiful Vision For Family?   41

A Beautiful Life?   48

A Beautiful Vision for Citizenship?   53

A Beautiful View of Humanity?   59

A Beautiful People (Known as The Church)?   66

A Beautiful vision of the Future?   73

Part Two: Is Christianity Believable?

Believable Truth?   80

A Believable Account of the Cosmos?   86

A Believable Account of Morality?   91

A Believable Account of Life?   95

A Believable Account of the Mind?   102

A Believable Account of Religion?   106

A Believable Explanation of Evil?   108

A Believable Explanation of the Bible?   114

A Believable Explanation Of Jesus?   120

A Believable Resurrection?   126

CONCLUSION   131

For Further Reading   133

About the Author   136

INTRODUCTION

The picture of the diving board on the cover was taken by one of my sons where we vacation. My sons have taken the plunge from this board many times. Me, not so much. I can understand reticence. However, despite my caution, there are good reasons to dive in from this board. The water is deep. There are no sharks. Jumping in can be great fun. Or so I am told. I tend to be a skeptical person.

There are many reasons people share for being skeptical of the claims of Christianity. In this short book I would like to introduce you to some reasons that we can lay aside our doubts and fears and take the plunge into a life of faith. It is beautiful. It is reasonable. And it can be great fun.

This book is presented in two parts. The first part gives reasons to believe in God and trust in Jesus based on the beauty of Christianity. The water is refreshing on a hot summer day. Jumping in is a beautiful experience. Christianity, when expressed well, leads to greater beauty in one's life, and indeed the world.

The second part gives reasons to believe in God and trust in Jesus despite the warnings of the people who say it is foolish to do so. According to the evidence, the water is deep, there are no sharks. Faith is not a blind leap, but a reasonable step.

If you are skeptical, I understand. However, I invite you to discover how Christianity is both beautiful and believable. I invite you to join me on the diving board, maybe we might even take a step . . .

PART ONE

IS CHRISTIANITY BEAUTIFUL?

If you have watched the tv show "A Handmaid's Tale" you will have seen a society built, supposedly, on Biblical rules. That society, called Gilead, is UGLY. Unfortunately, you don't need to have seen the show to know that Christianity can get ugly. Too many people know that first-hand.

For a faith perspective to be compelling, it must be beautiful. There will be a consistency between what it claims and where it leads. It would be strange if the evidence pointed to the existence of a good, just, and loving God, yet devotion to that God led to systems and traditions that promoted injustice and suffering. If Christianity is true, and reflects a good and loving God, we will expect it to bring beauty, not ugliness. Does it? We will consider this in the chapters to follow.

A BEAUTIFUL VIEW OF SCIENCE?

The relationship between faith and science has often turned ugly, sometimes devolving into a fight.

Should Christians be afraid of science? Should scientists be afraid of Christianity? We Canadians can typically be more science-focused than Bible-focused, even those of us who call ourselves Christians. When we Christians fall ill, do we follow James 5:14 and call the elders of the church, or do we call the doctor? As a pastor, I would be pleased to come and pray with you, but I will likely also encourage you to call the doctor if you have not already done so!

Do we learn from the Bible or science? Should we lean on, and into, the Bible, or science? Are we to choose between the two?

With this apparent conflict, and the potential for things to get ugly, what are we to think?

First, we should be aware that Christianity has provided a good foundation for science to flourish. Belief in a God who has ordered the universe and created laws that govern how things work inspires the investigation of how it all works. Christians have always been very much involved in science.

Second, we appreciate science for what it is, and what it is not. Science is the expectation that things operate according to patterns and laws which are predictable and discoverable. There is no argument with Christianity there. Science is therefore done without explicit reference to God, even when done by Christian scientists.

Let us consider a simple example of how science works. My youngest son once baked a rather large batch of very good peanut-butter cookies. I could run an experiment where I eat twenty cookies a day until they are all eaten, then step on the weigh scales to observe the effect of eating the cookies. If the rest of my eating patterns remained unchanged, we might predict a weight gain. Observation will confirm our theory. What we will not do is ask what God will do to my weight based on my cookie consumption. To do so would be to hold a "God of the gaps" kind of thinking, that is, that my weight gain is due to God, and not how my digestive system works. The experiment is not about finding God, but about finding how things work.

Science is the belief things operate according to laws. However, science is not the belief that there is no God. We Christians would say that science is the discovery of how God made things work. A Christian doing science does the same thing as an atheist doing science. Both are discovering how things operate. One speaks about the laws of nature, however they came about, the other of Creation operating according to God's design. Science is a methodology which does not seek God in the workings. To

say that science proves there is no God is not science, but a
faith perspective we can call *scientism*.

**Third, we appreciate what the Bible for what it is, and
what it is not.** The Bible is God's revelation of himself within
history with each part written to different people at different
times using different genres. The Bible is not a science
textbook written to science-minded Westerners. Of the
many genres used in the Bible, one genre you will not find is
a science lab report.

It is helpful to remember that the Bible was written for you,
but it was not written to you.[1] In Bible studies I have often
asked "what do you find striking in this passage?". We really
should ask how the passage would have struck the first
readers and hearers. What were the original readers meant
to learn, or what were they likely to learn?

To give an example, when the Book of Genesis was taking
shape people held that there were multiple gods who had
complicated relationships with each other, the world, and
humanity. The original hearers of what was written in the
Book of Genesis would have been struck by the fact there is
only one God worthy of consideration, that this God is a
God of order, the Creator of everything, and that this God
wants a relationship with all peoples, which will be worked
out in some way through one particular group of people,
the people descendant from a person named Israel. No one

---

[1] I do not remember where I first heard this distinction, but have found it
worth remembering!

would have questioned whether the universe really did come into existence fully formed in six literal 24 hour periods. That is a question we ask today when we fail to appreciate the theological poetry found in Genesis.

Fourth, we learn to navigate the relationship between science and Christianity as we follow the evidence. If our science and theology do not fit together, then either our understanding of theology is correct and our understanding of science is wrong, or, our understanding of science is correct and our understanding of theology is wrong. Or, it is a wee bit of both. Scientists are not infallible, their interpretations of, and inferences from, the data can be off. Bible teachers are not infallible, their interpretations of, and inferences from, the Bible can be off. With humility in our understanding of both science and theology we follow the evidence the best we can.

Turning to the Bible, let us consider John chapter 9. A blind man healed by Jesus was willing to follow the evidence. He was blind but then was healed. The evidence led him to the conclusion that Jesus is someone special. The Pharisees were also trying to follow the evidence in figuring out how the blind man was healed. However, they had prior assumptions which affected their conclusions:

> *The Jews didn't believe it, didn't believe the man was blind to begin with. So they called the parents of the man now bright-eyed with sight. They asked them, "Is this your son, the one you say was born blind? So how is it that he now sees?"*

His parents said, "We know he is our son, and we know he was born blind. But we don't know how he came to see—haven't a clue about who opened his eyes. Why don't you ask him? He's a grown man and can speak for himself." (His parents were talking like this because they were intimidated by the Jewish leaders, **who had already decided** *that anyone who took a stand that this was the Messiah would be kicked out of the meeting place. That's why his parents said, "Ask him. He's a grown man.")*
They called the man back a second time—the man who had been blind—and told him, "Give credit to God. **We know this man is an impostor**.*" John 9:18-24 (The Message, with emphasis added to point out the assumptions)*

The healed man did not begin with assumptions:

He replied, "I know nothing about that one way or the other. But I know one thing for sure: I was blind . . . I now see." John 9:25 (The Message)

Operating with different assumptions, the healed man could come to a very different conclusion about the identity of Jesus!

Science-minded people may come to an investigation of Jesus and the Bible with incorrect assumptions, and so miss the truth. They may have already decided that miracles cannot happen and therefore they have already concluded who they think Jesus is before they even begin their investigation. In doing so they can miss an amazing opportunity!

The shoe can be on the other foot, however. Notice that in John 9, it is the religious leaders who are the ones with the assumptions. The Christian may also hold assumptions about science and/or the Bible and so miss truth. In doing so the Christian can miss opportunities too.

Let us note where following the evidence led the man born-blind:

> *Jesus heard that they had thrown him out, and went and found him. He asked him, "Do you believe in the Son of Man?"*
> *The man said, "Point him out to me, sir, so that I can believe in him."*
> *Jesus said, "You're looking right at him. Don't you recognize my voice?"*
> *"Master, I believe," the man said, and worshiped him.*
> *John 9:35-38 (The Message)*

Do we need to pick between Christianity and science? Far from being in conflict, there is a good relationship between science and Christianity. One can follow the scientific evidence and be a Christian. In fact many people come to Christianity because of the evidence provided by science.

Many religions have fallen by the wayside, some would say thanks to science. However, Christianity is different. The fact that science can be in sync with Christian thinking reminds us that we need neither leave our brains at the door of the church, nor leave our faith in the parking lot of the university. When both are understood properly, there is a beautiful relationship between science and Christianity.

If Christianity caused us to abandon science we would be forced to turn our backs on so much that has helped humanity. That would be ugly. But there can be a good relationship between the two and that is part of what makes Christianity beautiful.

A BEAUTIFUL VISION FOR THOUGHT?

Can a thinking person be a Christian? Can a Christian be a thinking person? Is thinking discouraged within Christianity? I, for one, think that any religion that requires us to stop thinking is ugly. Is the Christian vision for thinking and thought beautiful, or ugly?

There is a lot of thinking going on in the Bible. We often find the Psalmists in deep thought:

> *"I remember the days of old, I think about all your deeds, I meditate on the works of your hands." Psalms 143:5 (NRSV)*
> *"On the glorious splendor of your majesty, and on your wondrous works, I will meditate." Psalms 145:5 (NRSV)*

There is also a whole portion of the Bible known as "Wisdom Literature" which is devoted to deep thinking. As examples, we find wisdom applied to life in Proverbs and deep contemplation in Ecclesiastes:

> *I, the Teacher, when king over Israel in Jerusalem, applied my mind to seek and to search out by wisdom*

all that is done under heaven . . . Ecclesiastes 1:12-13
(NRSV)

Thinking continues into the the New Testament:

> *As was his custom, Paul went into the synagogue, and on three Sabbath days he reasoned with them from the Scriptures, explaining and proving that the Messiah had to suffer and rise from the dead. "This Jesus I am proclaiming to you is the Messiah," he said. Some of the Jews were persuaded and joined Paul and Silas, as did a large number of God-fearing Greeks and quite a few prominent women. Acts 17:2-4 (NIV)*

Paul spent up to three years in Arabia following his conversion. Some Bible scholars believe this time was devoted to thinking through the results of Jesus' resurrection from the dead and how that event impacted religious thinking. With his extensive knowledge of the Old Testament, the startling revelation of the crucified, yet now alive, Jesus would have given him a lot to think about.

Second, there is a rich tradition of thinking throughout the history of Christianity. Some great thinkers throughout history include Augustine, Thomas Aquinas, Anselm, and Descartes to name a few. There are many great Christian thinkers in theology, but also in every other field of study including science, literature, and philosophy.

Many people come to a faith in Jesus through thinking. We can think, for example, of C.S. Lewis whose journey to Jesus was very thoughtful. We can think of Lee Strobel, who as a journalist came to Jesus through his journalistic enquiry into the truth about Christianity. We can also think about J. Warner Wallace, a cold-case detective who realised in reading the Gospels of Matthew, Mark, Luke, and John, that there was a ring of authenticity about these writings as witness accounts. He used his skills as a cold-case detective and that led him to faith in Jesus. In his podcasts Wallace has often lamented that people say they are Christians because they are raised in it, have some sort of experience through it, or find it helpful. Instead, he says that becoming a Christian is a reasonable step of following the evidence. Thinking can be the means God uses to draw us to him.

Many people come to a stronger faith through thinking. When I first expressed my sense of calling to be a pastor, one of the leaders of our Convention strongly encouraged me to not go to Bible College before my seminary training. Rather I was encouraged to earn a Bachelor of Arts or Science and be sure to take some philosophy and psychology. This turned out to be great advice.

While pursuing a Bachelor of Arts at Trent University my thinking about my faith was challenged. I came to the conclusion that if Christianity were true, it would also be reasonable. My faith in, and understanding of, God, has only deepened thanks to the exercise of thought. Indeed a church can be a place where people are encouraged to be thinking and thoughtful.

Yes, a thinking person can be a Christian, and a Christian can be, in fact ought to be, a thinking person. As we saw earlier, Christianity does not require us to leave our brains at the door of the church. Neither does Christianity require us to leave our faith in the university parking lot. A worldview or religion that asks us to do either would be ugly. The Christian vision for thought is beautiful.

A BEAUTIFUL VISION FOR RELIGION?

Religion can be ugly. Renowned atheist Christopher Hitchens is often quoted as saying "religion poisons everything." He had a valid point since religion has indeed destroyed many lives. If God is real, and God is love, then why does religion become so awful?

Yes, religion often poisons everything, some expressions of Christianity included. However, Christianity provides a compelling vision for religion.

Among various world-views there are different visions for religion, that is, what religion is supposed to do or accomplish.

Some religious people, Christians included, are focused on escape. The purpose of religion is to help you escape the troubles of this world and enter heaven, Nirvana, or some form of endless bliss.

Other religious people, Christians included, are focused on rules, regulations, and the consequences of obedience or disobedience. Sometimes those rules and regulations make no sense, but if a deity has given them, they must be obeyed no matter who gets hurt in the process. The purpose of this kind of religion is to keep people in line and ensure everyone gets what they deserve whether through bad karma or divine punishment.

So where should Christians find themselves in these two differing visions for religion?

Some will point to the apostle Paul's famous expression, "salvation by grace through faith" (Ephesians 2:8) and declare that escape is the vision for the Christian religion. The Christian will therefore say "I'm forgiven! I've got my golden ticket outta here!". Others will point to the famous expression of James, "faith without works is dead" (see James 2:17) and declare that the vision for the Christian religion is ensuring everyone keeps the rules. The Christian will therefore either say "We must do better at pleasing God." Do Paul and James have differing visions for religion? Which is correct?

The answer is neither. Both visions for religion miss the mark for what Christianity is about. Paul and James are not giving competing visions for religion, but rather they are looking at two different aspects of our relationship with God.

Let us consider an example from a marriage relationship. When Paul says of our relationship with God that "salvation is by grace through faith," it would be like Paul saying to me "you are married, not because you deserve your wife Sandra, nor because you decided you should be married, but because Sandra said 'yes.' She chose to be married to you!". When James says of our relationship with God that "faith without works is dead," it would be like James saying to me "if you don't spend any time with Sandra, if you pay her no attention whatsoever, if you ignore her, and you never help her, then your marriage is dead." We can think of Paul being focused on the engagement and the wedding day, while James is focused on how marriage is lived out every day since the wedding.

Now let us consider the two competing visions for religion we spoke of earlier.

Suppose my wife said to me on our wedding day, "I love you and want to be married to you today, but on the day in which you are less than perfect, we are done." I would not be married for very long! So too, a relationship with God that is focused on our performance would not last long at all.

Now suppose I said to my wife on our wedding day, "Go on the honeymoon without me," then on her return said "Good, I'm glad you are back, I now need to go on a fifty year mission trip and we will not be able to see each other until our 50th anniversary!" That would not be a marriage, that would be an arrangement. So too, if we are only focused on our technical standing before God, so as to get heaven someday, then we have an arrangement with God, not a relationship. Marriage is life-changing and is for life. The vision for religion as expressed by Christianity is a life-changing relationship with God that extends into eternity. This is neither escape, nor performance.

Paul and James are not promoting different visions for, or versions of, Christianity, they are speaking about different aspects of our relationship with God. What is the Christian vision for religion, then? An everlasting relationship with God that changes everything. We experience God's love in Jesus. We learn to love like Jesus. We experience God's life-changing presence through his Spirit. We learn to keep in step with the Spirit.

> *But the fruit of the Spirit is love, joy, peace, forbearance, kindness, goodness, faithfulness, gentleness and self-control. Against such things there is no law. Those who belong to Christ Jesus have crucified the flesh with its passions and desires. Since we live by the Spirit, let us keep in step with the Spirit. Galatians 5:22-25 NIV*

Religion is often about our reaching God. Christianity is about God reaching us, in fact reaching right into our hearts and massaging them back to life.

Many translations use the word religion in James 1:27:

> *Religion that God our Father accepts as pure and faultless is this: to look after orphans and widows in their distress and to keep oneself from being polluted by the world. James 1:27 NIV*

Here the Christian religion is far from poison, but a beautiful example of the expression of love, the fruit of the Spirit. It is what happens when there is a relationship with God. This is a very positive thing in our lives and in our world. Such a vision for religion is far more compelling than one that is focused merely on escape or obedience.

The Christian vision for religion is also more compelling than a vision of no religion at all. Some time ago atheist organizations placed ads on buses which said "There's probably no God. Now stop worrying and enjoy your life." But is it not better to worry about people who are suffering and in distress? Atheists usually recognise the need for goodness in our world, and will often seek to help others like religious people do. They would, however, be concerned if people actually took their advice and stopped worrying and just focused on enjoying themselves. Religion can poison everything. Atheism can poison everything too. A life-changing relationship with God, however, brings healing to a poisoned world.

The love of God enables us to enter into a life-changing, society-changing, world-changing covenant relationship with the Divine. Christianity provides a beautiful vision for religion which is consistent with a good and loving God.

A BEAUTIFUL VISION FOR A RELATIONSHIP WITH GOD?

Is the manner in which God relates to us beautiful? That is, does the relationship offered by God make us go "Wow, that makes sense and is is consistent with what we would expect from a good creator God."? Is it consistent with what the Bible teaches about God, namely that "God is love" (1 John 4:8)?

Many would answer, no. Their impression of Christianity is that you try to keep the rules, then you go to hell when you die because you couldn't. If that is it, then yes, it is very ugly indeed!

However, that's not it! Many religions are based on performance, that is, your relationship with God is dependent upon how well you keep the rules. Many people, including many Christians, think that Christianity is based on performance. That, however, is not Christianity.

What is Christianity? What does the Bible teach as to how God relates to us?

Let us go first to the Old Testament.

We might point to all the rules of the old covenant law and assume that one's relationship with God was, and is, based on performance. But look closer. Long before the law was given at a mountain called Mount Sinai, God was in relationship with humanity. Adam and Eve sinned, which introduced death and separation from God. However, God stayed in relationship with Adam and Eve, and with humanity. Israel was called to be a different kind of people, a people who followed God's lead. They often stumbled, and yes, bore the consequences. However, despite their poor performance, God stayed in relationship with stumbling Israel, and with stumbling humanity.

In the Bible we have a long record of relationship between God and humanity. Within this, to use literary language by way of analogy, the old covenant is a sub-plot which is essential to the unfolding of the main story. Yes, in the sub-plot Israel's performance was tied to Israel's future. If they rebelled against God, they would be exiled from the "promised land." They did rebel. They were exiled. But God stayed in relationship with them anyway! Through Israel God was working out his plan for relationship with all of us. That plan was not dependent on anyone's performance, but on God's desire, God's grace.

The old covenant law is not the main story, even of the Old Testament. The main story, from Genesis to Revelation, is God's relationship with humanity, not through our performance, but by His grace.

> . . . . *God, who saved us and called us with a holy calling, not according to our works but according to his own purpose and grace. This grace was given to us in Christ Jesus before the ages began, but it has now been revealed through the appearing of our Savior Christ Jesus, who abolished death and brought life and immortality to light through the gospel. 2 Timothy 1:8-10 (NRSV)*

Second, let us consider Jesus.

How do you begin your prayers? Is it "O all seeing, all knowing judge, who is ready to pounce on me for every sin"? Jesus, in teaching us to pray, taught us to begin with "Our Father." The Lord's Prayer begins in a manner which reminds us that we belong. We begin prayer with a reminder that when we are praying in the presence of God, we are exactly where we ought to be. We belong, even when we think that belonging is not what we deserve. In teaching us to pray, Jesus reminds us that we relate to God, not through our performance, but by God's grace.

Consider too, how Jesus related to people in the Gospels. Jesus was gracious to all, being known as a "friend of sinners"[2]. Jesus did have harsh words for some, namely the religious perfectionists who continually harped about performance of the law. Jesus modelled a grace-filled life. God relates to us in the same way Jesus related to people, not by our performance, but by his grace.

---

[2] see Matthew 11:19

Consider too, what we learn from Jesus' death on the cross. Basically, we killed God. He loved us anyway. That is all grace. Eternal life is a gift made possible by the grace of God.

Third, let us consider Paul, as an example of what the apostles taught.

Paul teaches about grace in Ephesians 2:1-10;

> *You were dead through the trespasses and sins in which you once lived, following the course of this world, following the ruler of the power of the air, the spirit that is now at work among those who are disobedient. All of us once lived among them in the passions of our flesh, following the desires of flesh and senses, and we were by nature children of wrath, like everyone else. But God, who is rich in mercy, out of the great love with which he loved us even when we were dead through our trespasses, made us alive together with Christ—by grace you have been saved— and raised us up with him and seated us with him in the heavenly places in Christ Jesus, so that in the ages to come he might show the immeasurable riches of his grace in kindness toward us in Christ Jesus. For by grace you have been saved through faith, and this is not your own doing; it is the gift of God— not the result of works, so that no one may boast. For we are what he has made us, created in Christ Jesus for good works, which God prepared beforehand to be our way of life. Ephesians 2:1-10 (NRSV emphasis added)*

Though we were in a mess, God rescued us. Paul himself is an example of grace, since he messed up terribly by persecuting people God was using to reach people with the good news of God's love. If God's grace can reach Paul, it can reach anyone.

How does God relate to us?

The Bible teaches that God's relationship with us is marked, not by the performance of perfect people, but by God's grace and love for imperfect people. This is a beautiful and compelling aspect of Christianity.

Grace provides a great atmosphere for our relationship with God. When a relationship is based on performance, it can be like sailing in a thunderstorm, scary. One never knows when lighting will strike. Perhaps one even feels that their mast is the tallest and will be the first to be struck. When a relationship is based on grace, it is like sailing with a good breeze on a sunny day. There can be adventure, enjoyment, and progress. Grace provides an atmosphere perfect for flourishing and growth.

When we receive God's grace, we do not come before Him like a distrusted employee before a cruel boss, or a hated criminal before a harsh judge. The Christian comes before God as an imperfect but growing child welcomed into the presence of a good, good parent. The Christian experience of grace is therefore consistent with how God would relate to us if "God is love." The manner in which God relates to us is consistent with a good and loving God. That is a beautiful thing.

A BEAUTIFUL VISION FOR OUR RELATIONSHIP WITH OTHERS?

For a worldview or religion to be compelling you would expect that it would lead to good relationships. This is especially true where offence is involved. Where there are relationships, there are hurting people, for people hurt people. We are human. If a worldview or religion is true, we should expect that it will help us relate to one another well and navigate these nasty quirks of our humanity. If God exists and loves us, we should expect that he will help us with something as important as relationships.

Does Christianity provide a beautiful and compelling vision for relationships including a method of dealing with offence? Some would say "No, Christianity is all about high expectations which makes people get all judgemental." Others would say, "No, Christianity is all about forgiveness which turns people into doormats." So which is it?

In the Last chapter we looked at the compelling way God relates to us. To summarise, God's relationship with us is based on His grace, not our performance. Now, how are we to relate to others?

Imitate God, therefore, in everything you do, because you are his dear children. Live a life filled with love, following the example of Christ. He loved us and offered himself as a sacrifice for us, . . . Ephesians 5:1-2 (NLT)

As God relates to us, we relate to others; with love and grace. Consider the following:

Dear friends, let us continue to love one another, for love comes from God. Anyone who loves is a child of God and knows God. But anyone who does not love does not know God, for God is love...
This is real love—not that we loved God, but that he loved us and sent his Son as a sacrifice to take away our sins. Dear friends, since God loved us that much, we surely ought to love each other....
God is love, and all who live in love live in God, and God lives in them. And as we live in God, our love grows more perfect. So we will not be afraid on the day of judgment, but we can face him with confidence because we live like Jesus here in this world.
Such love has no fear, because perfect love expels all fear. If we are afraid, it is for fear of punishment, and this shows that we have not fully experienced his perfect love. We love each other because he loved us first.
If someone says, "I love God," but hates a fellow believer, that person is a liar; for if we don't love people we can see, how can we love God, whom we cannot see? And he has given us this command:

We are to relate to others in the same manner God relates to us; with love and grace. There are some things we can say about this.

First, grace provides a compelling atmosphere for relationships. Some relationships are like walking on eggshells. Fear is constant. However, as we read above, "perfect love expels all fear." God drives out our fear for He does not treat us as our sins deserve (see Psalm 103), but rescues us and relates to us by his grace. What is true with our relationship with God can also be true in our relationship with others. Grace provides a great fear-free atmosphere where people can thrive in growing relationships. In marriage, in family, among friends, at the workplace, in teams, the experience of grace given-and-received provides a great atmosphere to live, work and play.

Second, grace provides a compelling response to offence. People often deal with offence by either "fight or flight." Neither work well and neither are to be the response of a Christian. Rather than lash out and risk an all out war, we are to turn the cheek. Some will say that is not at all compelling. Won't people walk all over us and take advantage of our grace? Well, no, grace provides for a flexibility in responding to offence.

Suppose a spouse is abused again and again, and each time the abused spouse is expected to forgive the abuser as if nothing ever happened. Is that compelling? No. I call this "doormat grace." Some would say this is the Christian vision for dealing with offence, but it is not.

The Bible teaches the need for grace, love, and forgiveness in relationships, yes, but the Bible also teaches the need for wisdom. The Book of Proverbs, a book full of wisdom, is still in the Bible! We need not offer doormat grace, but *wise* grace. Grace toward offenders means wanting the best for them, it does not mean putting up with the worst for yourself. When you respond with grace, you do not seek the destruction of the offender, but neither do you open yourself up for destruction. The gracious person turns the other cheek instead of hitting back. The wise person also takes a step back.

Grace, when applied with wisdom toward a serious and repeat offender, sounds like this: "I will not seek your harm even though I think you deserve it. However, I do not trust you and so have set boundaries so that you can not harm me further. There may be opportunities for changing these boundaries in the future, but right now I discern these to be appropriate for my own safety and well-being."

Grace leads to not seeking revenge. Wisdom considers the importance of trust and trustworthiness. Grace considers the possibility of future relationship. Wisdom considers the possibility of future harm. Grace leads to treating people better than they deserve. Wisdom leads to not letting people treat you worse than you deserve.

Grace in relationships is compelling and beautiful. It provides a great atmosphere for relationships and a compelling response to offence. Within Christian relationships there is space for growth, reconciliation, boundaries, and safety for oneself. Christianity when practised in emulation of God, in the Spirit of Christ, and keeping in step with the Holy Spirit, provides a beautiful vision for relationships. The manner in which Christians are to relate to others is consistent with a good and loving God. It is beautiful.

A BEAUTIFUL VISION OF GOD?

Is the God we meet in the Bible just? In being gracious and merciful, does God turn a blind eye to sin and injustice, and say "I just don't care"? We often rightly care about justice and have concern for those who experience injustice. Shouldn't God?

If a worldview or religion is to be beautiful, then won't justice be lifted up as important? Indeed a God that has no concern for justice is a God that does not love. If God is love, we will expect God to be perfect in his justice. A religion which promotes a God with no concern for justice is ugly.

So is the God of the Bible a God of justice?

We are introduced to the theme of justice very early in the Bible;

> *Then the Lord said to Cain, "Where is your brother Abel?"*
> *"I don't know, " he replied. "Am I my brother's keeper?"*
> *The Lord said, "What have you done? Listen! Your brother's blood cries out to me from the ground.*
> *Genesis 4:9-10 (NIV)*

We can assume that the blood of Abel was crying out, metaphorically speaking, to God for *justice*. Not too further along in the Old Testament we hear another cry for justice;

> *During that long period, the king of Egypt died. The Israelites groaned in their slavery and cried out, and their cry for help because of their slavery went up to God. God heard their groaning and he remembered his covenant with Abraham, with Isaac and with Jacob. So God looked on the Israelites and was concerned about them. Exodus 2:23-25 (NIV)*

The Hebrew for the last part literally and simply says "God saw the Israelites. He knew[3]." He knew they were experiencing injustice. Justice for Israel meant judgement for Egypt. In the plagues the Egyptians found out what it was like to be picked on, to receive what they had dealt out. The death of the firstborn males in the final plague mirrors the deaths of the Israelite male infants at the hands of the Egyptians. One is reminded of the Biblical "an eye for an eye, and a tooth for a tooth." Justice is held up as important.

We also find in the Book of Exodus a concern for God's people becoming a just society. The Book of Exodus moves at a very quick pace until the people reach Mount Sinai and everyone, and everything, comes to a stop. The fast-paced action ends and suddenly we find ourselves reading about

---

[3] I was first alerted to this literal translation by Peter Enns on the "Bible for Normal People" Podcast.

various legal matters, such as, what should happen if your ox gores someone.

Christians are not under the old covenant law as laid out in the Old Testament. However, Canadian Christians are under Canadian law. So if your neighbour's ox gores your friend, do not wave a Bible in their face, call the police! Our nation has laws in place to ensure it is a just society. Through the Old Testament civic laws, given to a specific people at a specific time, God was ensuring that the people rescued from the injustices of Egyptian society would themselves become a just society. If those laws seem like a tedious read, try reading the Canadian law books! Both are important for the existence of a just society.

In many ways, the laws given to Israel signalled a step forward from other ancient societies with regards to justice. There were laws to ensure that no one goes hungry, that the vulnerable were taken care of, that foreigners were treated fairly, and that no child was sacrificed for religious purposes as was happening in some of the surrounding societies. Indeed, a concern for justice rings throughout the entire Bible.

While I originally planned that the title of this chapter would be "A Beautiful Vision for Justice," I went with "A Beautiful Vision of God" instead. Why? Because in Jesus the justice of God and the mercy of God come together in a beautiful and compelling way. Consider these verses from Isaiah:

> *Surely he took up our pain*

and bore our suffering,
yet we considered him punished by God,
stricken by him, and afflicted.
But he was pierced for our transgressions,
he was crushed for our iniquities;
the punishment that brought us peace was on him,
and by his wounds we are healed.
We all, like sheep, have gone astray,
each of us has turned to our own way;
and the Lord has laid on him
the iniquity of us all. Isaiah 53:4-6 (NIV)

While these verses probably referred originally to God's people, they became meaningful to Jesus followers as pointing out the role of Jesus when it comes to God's justice.

For God to be considered just, there must be a consequence for sin. Sin cannot simply be wafted away as being unimportant. Yet for God to be considered merciful, our sin must be lifted from us somehow, for no one is without sin. We have no future in God's presence without mercy. In Christ, God has been merciful in taking away our sin, and yet just, by dealing with it at the same time. "The Lord has laid on him the iniquity of us all." Keeping in mind that Jesus is the incarnation of God, God the Son, God Himself has been both merciful and just by bearing the punishment we deserve.

In this bringing together of justice and mercy, Christianity is unique among all the religions of the world. As Peter points out in his sermon as recorded in the Book of Acts,

> *Salvation is found in no one else, for there is no other name under heaven given to mankind by which we must be saved. Acts 4:12 (NIV)*

Salvation is found in no one else because there is no one else who could bring justice and mercy together as God has done in Jesus. There is no one else who could have done for us what God Himself could do for us. There is no one else who has done for us what God Himself has done for us.

God is consistent in his justice and mercy. Some people think that God was all justice in the Old Testament, but all merciful in the New. However, the Old Testament is a record of people experiencing both the justice and mercy of God. The New Testament is also a record of people experiencing the justice and mercy of God. God will be experienced as a God of both perfect justice and mercy in the future.

What will be the focus in your future?

Will you experience the justice of a merciful God? He will not force you to spend eternity with him if that is something you don't want. He will do the right thing, the just thing. No one will say "that is not fair" when those who reject God find themselves no longer in his presence in any way.

However, God is merciful and it does not need to end that way.

Will you experience the mercy of a just God? We will not spend eternity with God on our own merit. Yet "by his bruises we are healed." God will do a really good thing. He will show mercy, yet in Jesus it will be consistent with his just nature.

Any religion that presents God as either lacking in justice, or lacking in mercy, is not beautiful. The God we meet in the Bible, revealed supremely in Jesus, is the God of justice and mercy. This is a beautiful vision of who God is.

A BEAUTIFUL ENGAGEMENT WITH NON-CHRISTIANS?

Does the way in which Christians are directed to reach out to people outside of Christianity point to the reality of God? Is the engagement with others beautiful, or ugly? Some might immediately think of the Spanish inquisition, or their own personal inquisition in the presence of a zealous and chatty Christian who is intent on forcing Christianity down their throat. While people may not normally run from Christians, they may run from Christians they perceive to be on a mission! However, what we call "Christian mission" is beautiful for the following reasons.

First, freedom is beautiful. Imprisonment is always an ugly thing. With Christianity there is to be freedom. When we read the New Testament we find people freely choosing to be followers of Jesus. In the "Great Commission" of Matthew 28, Jesus did not say "go and force everyone to be a Christian," but "go and make disciples."

This means that everyone should have freedom *to not be* a Christian. Some religions and world-views use power to keep people in. We can think of fundamentalist versions of

Islam. In some nations it is illegal to convert from Islam to another faith. My own children have been raised with a strong connection with the church family. But they are free to not be Christians. While my heart's desire is that all three will follow Jesus, it is not my decision to make. They are free to choose their spirituality. As they grow into adulthood they will be free to also choose their connection with the church family. Sometimes we as Christians have made it difficult for people to leave the faith. That gets ugly. Freedom is beautiful.

There is also to be freedom for the non-Christian to not act like a Christian. Jesus did not say in Matthew 28 "go and make Christian nations, forcing everyone to have Christian morals," but,

> . . . go and make disciples of all the nations, baptizing them in the name of the Father and the Son and the Holy Spirit. 20 **Teach these new disciples** to obey all the commands I have given you. And be sure of this: I am with you always, even to the end of the age." Matthew 28:19-20 (NLT emphasis added)

The New Living Translation goes beyond what is in the original Greek, but captures well for us who are to learn Christ's ways, namely, his disciples. As a Canadian I have been watching the culture war in the States with interest. It seems that along with a desire to "make America great again" was a desire to 'make America Christian again.' However, forcing an entire nation to follow Jesus gets ugly. We are given to understand that Christianity is spreading like a virus in China. I imagine that the Chinese Christians are not fighting a culture war, but are focused on making disciples, one person at a time. That is not to say that Christians can not and should not be involved in politics. But when we are, let us not confuse making laws with making disciples.

We Christians have sometimes denied freedom to others, and sometimes still do. It has been and still is ugly. But we will not deny freedom if we are looking to Jesus, if the New Testament is our guide. Freedom is beautiful, and a Biblical Christianity promotes freedom.

Second, words are a beautiful way to share truth. Forced conversion through violence is ugly. Conversion through force or manipulation is something you will not find happening in the New Testament, nor is it something Jesus told us to do. Instead, we find people sharing what they knew to be true about Jesus simply by using good words and good deeds. You will not find a Christian going to war in the New Testament to 'take the land for Jesus.' You will find honest sharing. You will find conversations. You will not find warriors. You will find preachers, teachers, and people living quiet, but profoundly Christian, lives.

We Christians have sometimes resorted to power, and sometimes we still do. That is ugly. However, we will not use force if we are looking to Jesus, if the New Testament is our guide. It has been said that the pen is mightier than the sword. It is also a more beautiful method of reaching out to others. A Biblical Christianity promotes conversation and sharing through words and action.

Third, it is a beautiful thing to share good news. Keeping life-changing good news to oneself would be ugly. Keeping Jesus for ourselves would be ugly. Keeping quiet about the amazing news of God's amazing grace would be ugly. Some religions may promote a 'keep it to yourself' attitude. That might be okay if you are keeping your love for liver and onions to yourself. But imagine finding the cure for cancer. It would be cruel to keep that to yourself. In Christ we have learned of the cure for death itself! We have learned that God has a love solution for our separation-from-God problem. Keeping that to ourselves would demonstrate an ugly, ugly lack of love for others. From the very earliest days, Christians have been involved in helping people come to know Jesus. Do we do share Jesus with others so that we can get to heaven? Nope! We share because sharing good news is a beautiful thing, a natural thing. The good news is too good to keep to ourselves.

The way Christians are to engage non-Christians is not ugly, but beautiful. Freedom is beautiful, words are a beautiful way to share truth, and sharing good news is beautiful. God's call for how the Christian should engage with the non-Christian is beautiful, just as you would expect from a good God.

A BEAUTIFUL VISION FOR FAMILY?

Does Christianity have a compelling and beautiful vision for family life? Some ancient religions required child sacrifice. That is not a beautiful vision for family at all! Some would say that the Christian vision for family is likewise ugly. It is too rigid and too patriarchal. Does the Christian vision for family make you think "that sounds right, that is consistent with a good and loving God"? Is the Biblical vision for family beautiful, or ugly? It is beautiful, for the following reasons.

There is a beautiful vision for parenting.

To begin with, child sacrifice was strictly forbidden under the Old Covenant law. God's people were to be different from other peoples of that day who did indeed sacrifice their children. The place near Jerusalem where people sacrificed their children was eventually used as a garbage dump as it was despised by God's people. It was called Gehenna, which many English Bibles translate as 'hell.' God's people were expressly forbidden from sacrificing their children. This already was a positive step for family life!

But are there any other good parenting tips beyond "don't sacrifice your children"? If you happened to read through the entire Bible this week, you might say, "I did not see too much on parenting." If parenting is all about technique, then no, the Bible does not say much. However, if parenting is about character, then the Bible has much to say. Let us consider one example from Galatians:

> *The acts of the flesh are obvious: sexual immorality, impurity and debauchery; idolatry and witchcraft; hatred, discord, jealousy, fits of rage, selfish ambition, dissensions, factions and envy; drunkenness, orgies, and the like. I warn you, as I did before, that those who live like this will not inherit the kingdom of God. Galatians 5:19-21 (NIV)*

Not only will those who "live like this" not inherit the kingdom of God, they will also make life miserable for their children! Let us read what comes next:

> *But the fruit of the Spirit is love, joy, peace, forbearance, kindness, goodness, faithfulness, gentleness and self-control. Against such things there is no law. Those who belong to Christ Jesus have crucified the flesh with its passions and desires. Galatians 5:22-24 (NIV)*

Those who live like this will be appreciated by their children! Who wouldn't want to grow up with parents whose character is marked by love, joy, peace, patience, kindness, goodness, faithfulness, gentleness, and self control? Techniques in parenting will vary according to culture, but the good character of a parent can make for beautiful parenting in any society.

Character development is also good for marriage, which is also great for family life. This brings us to our second point.

There is a beautiful vision for marriage.

While we find polygamy quite often in the Old Testament, things are different in the New Testament. In speaking about marriage, Jesus focused, not on the people from the Old Testament who practiced polygamy, nor on the law, which allowed for polygamy, but on the creation account:

> Some Pharisees came to him to test him. They asked, "Is it lawful for a man to divorce his wife for any and every reason?"
> "Haven't you read," he replied, "that at the beginning the Creator **'made them male and female,'** and said, **'For this reason a man will leave his father and mother and be united to his wife, and the two will become one flesh'**? So they are no longer two, but one flesh. Therefore what God has joined together, let no one separate." Matthew 19:3-6 (NIV. Quotations from Genesis emphasized)

This return to the original vision for marriage paved the way for women to be on a more equal footing. Polygamy naturally leads to someone being in charge of "the clan," a supreme leader. Monogamy more naturally allows for the possibility of an equal partnership.

Further, the Biblical vision is of covenant faithfulness and loyal love between two people. Such covenant faithfulness, based on God's covenant faithfulness, is a beautiful thing and enables family life to be settled and stable. It is a beautiful thing to grow up in a home where one's parents are in love,...with each other!

There is also a beautiful vision for leadership and submission in marriage:

> *Submit to one another out of reverence for Christ. Wives, submit yourselves to your own husbands as you do to the Lord. For the husband is the head of the wife as Christ is the head of the church, his body, of which he is the Savior. Now as the church submits to Christ, so also wives should submit to their husbands in everything.*
> *Husbands, love your wives, just as Christ loved the church and gave himself up for her to make her holy, cleansing her by the washing with water through the word, and to present her to himself as a radiant church, without stain or wrinkle or any other blemish, but holy and blameless. Ephesians 5:21-27 (NIV)*

Perhaps that does not sound beautiful to everyone. Women being under the thumb of a controlling man sounds ugly. Indeed it is. However, let us dig deeper. When leadership is about control, it is ugly. When leadership is about care and responsibility, it is beautiful. Notice the focus on the lengths Jesus went to in his care of, and love for, the Church. He was willing to die for the Church! There was a great expectation placed by Paul on men here to love sacrificially, an expectation which was not prevalent in that day.

Likewise, when submission is about giving control over, it can be ugly. When submission is about trust, it is beautiful. When a man loves a woman the way Christ loves the church, trust is built.

This passage is not about men taking control without building any trust. It is about harmony between two people in care and trust. It is a beautiful vision that was quite radical and affirming of women when it was first written. Let us not forget verse 21, "Submit to one another out of reverence for Christ." Love, trust, and mutual submission makes for great family life.

There is beautiful flexibility in the Christian vision for Family.

Although Jesus focused in on the creation account of marriage, something you do not find in the New Testament is a push for everyone to be married with children. Jesus himself affirmed that not everyone will be married with children in Matthew 19:10-12[4]. The Ethiopian eunuch, who did not fit the mould of "married with children" was welcomed into the Kingdom in Acts chapter 8. Paul encouraged people to remain single in 1st Corinthians

---

[4] "Some, from birth seemingly, never give marriage a thought. Others never get asked—or accepted. And some decide not to get married for kingdom reasons. But if you're capable of growing into the largeness of marriage, do it." Matthew 19:12 (The Message)

chapter 7, or to get married! There is flexibility! While married with children is a beautiful vision, it was not an expectation in the New Testament church. It should not become an idol in ours. If you are single, or have no children, you are not a second class citizen in the Kingdom of God. No one should feel like second class citizen in a church because of they are not married with children. No one should feel like second class citizen in a church period.

Since there is flexibility in not forcing everyone to fit the pattern of married with children as set out in the creation account, is there also flexibility with leadership within the family? Can it be based on giftedness and capacity rather than gender as Paul indicated in the passage quoted above? My wife takes the lead in a number of areas of our family life. She is *so* much more capable than I am in many things! Let us remember that Paul was writing to a people steeped in a patriarchal way of doing things. Many of us take Paul's writing as a signpost along the way toward a more equal future, rather than the final destination.

Continuing to think about equality, Proverbs, chapter 31, is often thought to be about "the virtuous wife." It is often pitched to women, that they should be more like that ideal woman. However, I think it was written for men. The lesson of Proverbs 31 for men can be summed up as "don't micro-manage your wife, she excels without your interference." Proverbs ends with this instruction:

Honor her for all that her hands have done,

and let her works bring her praise at the city gate.
Proverbs 31:31 (NIV)

This description of the capability of a woman must also be considered a part of the overall Biblical vision for family. The flexibility of the Biblical vision for family is a beautiful thing.

As the father of an openly gay child I also have to wonder if the flexibility also extends to the nature of marriage covenant as exclusively between a man and a woman. I have seen a gay marriage that was beautiful. I have also seen the ugliness of Christians fighting about it. This is an important question which affects people deeply.

There are those who say that even if they became convinced that Christianity is true, they would still not want to be a Christian because it has a very patriarchal, homophobic, transphobic, and constrictive vision for family life. Indeed, some Christians live out a constrictive and patriarchal vision and expect others to do likewise. However, digging deeper into the writings of the Bible we discover a vision for family which is beautiful in its vision and flexibility. It is indeed consistent with a good and loving God.

A BEAUTIFUL LIFE?

Is the kind of life Christianity leads to beautiful, or ugly? If God is good, then we would expect the way God would have us live should bring beauty and not ugliness. So does it?

Some would say no. In the Margaret Atwood novel, A Handmaid's Tale, everything is supposedly ordered according to the Bible. It does not take too long for the reader to figure out that this is a very ugly society. Many would say that even without the kind of state control found in the novel, the Christian life is ugly. It is thought of as blindly following many, many rules without any thought as to whether they are good or not.

So is the Christian life beautiful or ugly? People may portray the Christian life as ugly, or even point to a Christian who is living out a life that is ugly, but the writings of the Bible point to a life that is beautiful for the following reasons.

First, the Christian life is a Jesus-centred life.

> *And Jesus came and said to them, "All authority in heaven and on earth has been given to me. Go therefore and make disciples of all nations, baptizing them in the name of the Father and of the Son and of the Holy Spirit, and teaching them to obey everything that I have commanded you. And remember, I am with*

The focus *was not* to be on what the teachers of the law commanded in Jesus' day. The focus *is not* to be on what the teachers of the law command in ours. The focus is on Jesus and what he commanded. It is not about powerful people or powerful traditions. It is about Jesus.

The focus is on Jesus, even when we are reading the letters of Paul, Peter, James, John, or Jude. The letters of the New Testament are not "here is something new, because Jesus did not say enough," but rather, "here are the implications of Jesus on our thinking, and here is what the Jesus-focused life looks like for us in our day." What we have in the letters are the apostles working out the implications of Jesus for first century Rome, Corinth, Ephesus, and so on.

This has important implications. Take slavery, for example. Some would say that the inclusion of slavery in the New Testament demonstrates that the Christian life is ugly. Does the New Testament support the institution of slavery? Slavery was a normal part of life in that day, a fact which was not going to change anytime soon. Since slavery was a normal part of life, Paul offered how a Jesus-centred person should live when they happen to be a slave, or be a slave holder. In fact, there are beautiful implications as we discover in Paul's letter to Philemon where Philemon is encouraged to take back his runaway slave, Onesimus, "no longer as a slave but more than a slave, a beloved brother" (Philemon 16 NRSV). Philemon's Jesus-focused life would be a thing of beauty for Onesimus. Life is beautiful when it is impacted by Jesus, even when society is stuck in ugliness.

We do not read Paul's letters to find out how to become a Paul follower, or how to be more focused on Paul in our lives. We read Paul's letters to discover how people were encouraged to be Jesus followers, to live Jesus-centred lives in the first century. This helps us discover how we can live Jesus-focused lives in our day.

A Jesus-centred life is a beautiful life. Of course this is so, Jesus was a beautiful person! Notice the way he related to people, his integrity, his reverence for the Divine, his focus on the spirit of the law and not the letter, his ability to challenge and unravel the status quo, his living out of the great commandments of love for God and neighbour, and his good works. Notice how he offers life to those who took his. Jesus is beautiful. A Jesus-centred life is a beautiful life.

Second, the Christian life is a Spirit filled life.

> By contrast, **the fruit of the Spirit is love, joy, peace, patience, kindness, generosity, faithfulness, gentleness, and self-control.** There is no law against such things. And those who belong to Christ Jesus have crucified the flesh with its passions and desires. If we live by the Spirit, let us also be guided by the Spirit. Galatians 5:22-25 (NRSV emphasis added)

The "fruit of the Spirit" is all beautiful stuff! We would describe a person whose character is marked by such traits as being a beautiful person.

Fruit grows naturally. A beautiful character is the natural consequence of a relationship with God. Fruit naturally grows where the conditions are right. Our part is to see that the conditions are good by keeping our connection with God open through prayer, thoughtful reading of the Scriptures, relationships with other Christians (especially those who are more mature in bearing spiritual fruit than us), and worship. But God is the One who makes fruit grow. A Spirit filled life is a beautiful life.

Third, the Christian life is a life of wisdom.

> *Who is wise and understanding among you? Show by your good life that your works are done with gentleness born of wisdom. But if you have bitter envy and selfish ambition in your hearts, do not be boastful and false to the truth. Such wisdom does not come down from above, but is earthly, unspiritual, devilish. For where there is envy and selfish ambition, there will also be disorder and wickedness of every kind. But the wisdom from above is first pure, then peaceable, gentle, willing to yield, full of mercy and good fruits, without a trace of partiality or hypocrisy. And a harvest of righteousness is sown in peace for those who make peace. James 3:13-18 (NRSV emphasis added)*

The New Testament letter of James has been described by some Biblical scholars as being like the "wisdom literature" we find in the Old Testament. It points to the good life and how to live well. Notice the focus in the quoted passage on gentleness and peace. The wise person knows that being gentle and peaceable is a good thing. A wise person living in wisdom is a beautiful thing. A life of wisdom is a beautiful life.

Conclusion.

Some paint the Christian life as being ugly. It is portrayed as blindly following rules without any thought given as to whether those rules are helpful or not. It is portrayed as a very narrow life with no fun allowed at all. But that's not it! The Christian is to be Jesus-centred, Spirit filled, and wise! The Christian life is a beautiful life, just as we should expect if Christianity is true, if God is good.

A BEAUTIFUL VISION FOR CITIZENSHIP?

Are Christians to rebel against reigning governments or submit to them? Are Christians to take over governments? Does the Christian vision for society lead to a theocracy, where God's law is the law of the land? Does Christianity promote a beautiful vision for society? If God is real, and Christianity is true, then we should expect beauty and not ugliness in the vision for citizenship. What is the vision?

Are Christians to rebel?

> *So they called the apostles back in and commanded them never again to speak or teach in the name of Jesus.*
> *But Peter and John replied, "**Do you think God wants us to obey you rather than him**? We cannot stop telling about everything we have seen and heard."*
> *Acts 4:18-20 (NLT emphasis added)*

> *The captain went with his Temple guards and arrested the apostles, but without violence, for they were afraid the people would stone them. Then they brought the apostles before the high council, where the high priest confronted them. "We gave you strict orders*

*never again to teach in this man's name!" he said.
"Instead, you have filled all Jerusalem with your
teaching about him, and you want to make us
responsible for his death!"*
*But Peter and the apostles replied, "**We must obey
God rather than any human authority**." Acts 5:26-29
(NLT emphasis added)*

In the New Testament we find rebellion against the
authorities in order to be obedient to God. We can think of
many Christians around the world who disobey the
authorities by gathering together as Christians, by telling
others about Jesus, and sometimes simply by owning a
Bible. May those of us who are Christians in lands of greater
freedom be in prayer for the underground Church around
the world. So yes, we are encouraged to rebel and break
the laws when necessary.

So therefore Christians should never submit?

> ***Everyone must submit to governing authorities.*** *For
> all authority comes from God, and those in positions
> of authority have been placed there by God. So
> anyone who rebels against authority is rebelling
> against what God has instituted, and they will be
> punished. For the authorities do not strike fear in
> people who are doing right, but in those who are
> doing wrong. Would you like to live without fear of the
> authorities? Do what is right, and they will honor you.
> The authorities are God's servants, sent for your good.
> But if you are doing wrong, of course you should be*

afraid, for they have the power to punish you. They are God's servants, sent for the very purpose of punishing those who do what is wrong. So you must submit to them, not only to avoid punishment, but also to keep a clear conscience.Pay your taxes, too, for these same reasons. For government workers need to be paid. They are serving God in what they do. Give to everyone what you owe them: Pay your taxes and government fees to those who collect them, and give respect and honor to those who are in authority.
Romans 13:1-7 (NLT emphasis added)

Keep in mind that these words are taken from Paul's letter to Rome, the seat of power in the ancient world. While the Christians in Rome recognised that saying "Jesus is Lord" meant therefore saying that Caesar is not, there was still a call to respect the authorities. There is an impulse to be good citizens of the land, to be good Romans when in Rome, or a good Canadian when in Canada.

We therefore find in the New Testament a balance between respect for the authorities as good citizens of the land, but also disobedience when necessary.

Are Christians to take over the government, to aim for a "Christian Nation," or to establish a theocracy?

Reading through the entire New Testament we find no encouragement to take over the government or to establish a theocracy. Christianity began as a minority movement and therefore a takeover was not even entertained as a possibility. Even so, neither do we find a longing to do so at some point in the future when we have enough influence. What we find is a focus on individuals having a life-changing encounter with Christ. We find disciples making disciples. We find the recognition that Jesus already reigns without the need for a political or military coup. There is no need to take over the government, for Jesus is already Lord. There is no need to set up a theocracy, for God is already sovereign.

> *Then the seventh angel blew his trumpet, and there were loud voices shouting in heaven:*
> *"The world has now become the Kingdom of our Lord and of his Christ,*
> *and he will reign forever and ever." Revelation 11:15 (NLT)*

The place of the Christian is not to enforce laws that make the land look like God's kingdom. The place of the Christian is to live kingdom focused lives while watching and waiting for God to bring the Divine kingdom.

We find something similar in Old Testament. While there was a call for the establishment of a theocracy, known as Israel, there was no impulse for that theocracy to take over the world. Israel was not called to take over the world, but to be salt and light *to* the world. Christians today are to be salt and light *within* the world.

We are to have influence on society, but we are to be salt and light, not a hammer and gun. We are to carry a cross, not a sword. Helping people know Jesus is the priority of the Christian, not enforcing non-Christian people to live like Christians, especially not our own vision of what a Christian looks like. Sometimes a person's idea of "theocracy," a term referring to God being the leader, might better be termed "me-ocracy." We are not to be kings over the land but kingdom people in the land, leading kingdom lives, looking forward to the Kingdom to come. We are disciples making disciples.

As lives are changed, society is changed. Christianity has brought good and beautiful changes to society, yet it is to do so without a vision for totalitarian control. We can consider how Christianity has nurtured human rights.

As an interesting example, consider the nations that are the best, and those that are the worst, to live in if you are gay. According to one source[5], here are the ten best nations to live in if you are gay in ascending order; Argentina, Belgium, Malta, Germany, Iceland, Portugal, Sweden, The Netherlands, Spain, and Canada. My own nation of Canada takes the top spot as the best! From another source[6], here are the worst in descending order; Afghanistan, Sudan, Yemen, Iran, Saudi Arabia, Somaliland, Nigeria, Russia, United Arab Emirates, and Mauritania. Notice anything about these two lists? The nations that are considered best have all had Christianity working in the background for a long time, helping to shape the culture, helping to develop

---

[5] https://nomadicboys.com/most-gay-friendly-countries-in-the-world/

[6] https://www.worldatlas.com/articles/10-worst-countries-for-lgbt-rights.html

a societal vision of love for one's neighbour and an appreciation of human rights. The nations that are considered worst share a history of either sharia law or communism, strict Islam or atheism. Rights and freedoms have flourished in lands that have been marinating in Christianity. This speaks positively about the relationship between Christianity and society.

To conclude, the New Testament does not promote a vision for society that is to be fought for, that is to be enforced. That would get ugly quite quickly. Unfortunately, being all too human, we Christians have made things get ugly at times.

What the New Testament promotes is a vision for how Christians engage with and interact within society, any society. We are to be individuals reaching individuals with the good news of the love of God as expressed in Jesus Christ. We are to be disciples making disciples. We are to do good, to love our neighbours. We are to lead Jesus-centred, Spirit-filled, wisdom-seeking lives. We are to be kingdom people living kingdom lives, while watching and waiting for the kingdom to come. We are to be good citizens of whatever land we live in. We are to rebel when necessary.

Overall, the Christian Scriptures promote a beautiful vision for how Christians engage with and live within society. This is consistent with what we would expect from a good and loving God.

A BEAUTIFUL VIEW OF HUMANITY?

Does Christianity lead to a beautiful perspective on humanity? Or is it ugly? If the God of the Bible is real, and is love, then we should expect beauty and not ugliness. Some would say it is ugly, setting up some people as better than the rest, creating a people who look down on others. It sets up a hierarchy of worth and value. It sets up some humans, perhaps most, or all according to some, as being worthless. There is no doubt, that we, who are Christians, have sometimes acted or spoken like this is so. But is that accurate? What do the Christian Scriptures teach about the Christian perspective on humanity?

Let us turn first, to the beginning;

> *Then God said, "Let us make human beings in our image, to be like us. . . . .*
> *So God created human beings in his own image.*
> *In the image of God he created them;*
> *male and female he created them. Genesis 1:26-27 (NLT)*

All people are created in the image of God, without exception. This fact unites us in our humanity.

It might be suggested that while this was true of Adam and Eve, it has not been true of anyone since the Fall, that we no longer bear the image of God because of sin. However, consider this early appeal to justice;

> *"And I will require the blood of anyone who takes another person's life. If a wild animal kills a person, it must die. And anyone who murders a fellow human must die. If anyone takes a human life, that person's life will also be taken by human hands. For God made human beings in his own image. Genesis 9:5-6 (NLT)*

To paraphrase, "how dare you lift a finger against another person in violence, for all people were created in the image of God and that still matters even though you are no longer in the Garden of Eden." Every person has worth and value.

Now let us turn to the ending;

> *After this I saw **a vast crowd, too great to count, from every nation and tribe and people and language**, standing in front of the throne and before the Lamb. They were clothed in white robes and held palm branches in their hands. And they were shouting with a great roar,*
> *"Salvation comes from our God who sits on the throne and from the Lamb!" . . . .*
> *Then he said to me, "These are the ones who died in the great tribulation. They have washed their robes in the blood of the Lamb and made them white.*
> *"That is why they stand in front of God's throne*

The Book of Revelation speaks of an incredible diversity of peoples gathered together in Jesus. From this we learn that all people have the opportunity to know God.

To sum up what we learn at both the beginning and end of the Bible, we will never meet a person who was not created in the image of God, and we will never meet a person for whom Jesus did not choose to bear the cross. All people bear the image of God without exception. Without exception, Jesus bore the cross for all people. That is the starting point for a Christian's relationship with others. It is to be our perspective on humanity.

We see this humanity-valuing perspective in the writings of the Bible, not only at the beginning and the end, but also from beginning to end. For example,

- When Abraham is called, that calling is ultimately for the sake of all nations, not just Abraham's descendants.

- In the Old Testament there are laws that provide for the well-being of the foreigner.

- Foreigners were welcomed into the community, as exemplified with The Book of Ruth. While the practice of foreign religion among the Israelites was unacceptable, foreign people were accepted.

- God's concern for the foreigner was made explicitly clear in The Book of Jonah. Jonah shrank back from God's call to preach to the enemy, the people of Ninevah, because he knew and was disgusted that God would be kind to them. God did indeed show His kindness to them.

- Jesus loved all kinds of people, even touching "unclean" people, whom no one would ever dare touch, before healing them.

- Jesus taught the importance of love for the neighbour, then emphasised that the neighbour is anyone and everyone. Your neighbour could even be those dreaded Samaritans, who can act better than the religious elites by the way, as Jesus pointed out in the Parable of the Good Samaritan.

- God called Phillip for a special mission to the Ethiopian eunuch, who was from a different land, likely had a different skin colour from Phillip, and, being a eunuch, could be described as having a different sexuality.

- God gave the Holy Spirit to all kinds of people beyond the Jewish people.

From beginning to end, the Bible promotes the value and worth of all people. This covers more than just race, it covers any kind of difference. Consider that in a very patriarchal time and place, there is an emphasis on the equality of the sexes;

> *So God created human beings in his own image.*
> *In the image of God he created them;*
> *male and female he created them. Genesis 1:26-27*
> *(NLT)*

Speaking of gender, there is a lot going on with gender in society these days. Some of us may struggle to understand why a man identifies as a woman, or a woman as a man, or why some don't identify as either. The starting point for relationship, even when people are beyond our understanding, is this: they are created in the image of God and Jesus chose to bear the cross for them. What will we choose to do for them?

All people bear the image of God without exception. Without exception, Jesus bore the cross for all people. This is true for people who are unique for any reason.

With each of our pregnancies, my wife and I were offered the opportunity to test for Down syndrome. This would lead to an opportunity to have an abortion. In our minds people with Down syndrome have as much worth and value as any other person. They are created in the image of God. Jesus chose the cross for them. Therefore should a Christian carry on with such a test?

Speaking of abortion, in my mind, a person in the womb has as much value and worth as a person outside of the womb. This is why Christians often tend to be pro-life. We should understand that nothing is as simple as it seems, that there is a great need for sensitivity on this topic, and people need reminding of the grace of God. Also, we should understand that some people are pro-choice based on their Christian ethic, based on love and concern for moms and women in difficult circumstances. Nevertheless, every person has value and the question is valid; is a fetus just "tissue," or a person created in the image of God and for whom Jesus bore the cross? I raise this, not to end the conversation, but to begin it.

Given that all humanity bears the image of God, the Christian can not look down on any person as being worth less for any reason. Rather, we are called to love others with the love of Christ who bore the cross for them. The starting point is not "you are so different from me," but "we are so much alike, in that we are all created in the image of God and we all receive an invitation for relationship with the Divine." All people bear the image of God without exception. Without exception, Jesus bore the cross for all people. This is the Christian view of humanity, and it is beautiful.

Now consider what can happen when we take God out of the picture. Without the Biblical perspective on humanity, we can easily fall into racism, sexism, or looking down on people because they are different. If we are indeed the product of unguided evolution, if there is no God, then what is to stop us from thinking that one race has greater value than another? The rat has had just as much time to evolve as the human. We naturally give the human more value and will call exterminators to deal with rat infestations so as to protect humans from disease. What is to stop us from giving greater value to one type of human, even going as far as exterminating other types of humans to protect the "more valuable"? Indeed this kind of thing has happened throughout history. It was not Bible study and a hunger for God that led the Nazi war machine to commit atrocities against the Jews. It was philosophical thinking that applied evolution to society. "We are more highly evolved than you" is ugly. In contrast, "You bear the image of God, Christ bore the cross for you," is beautiful.

Every single person bears the image of God, regardless of colour, culture, medical conditions, gender, sexuality, or anything else. Jesus bore the cross for every person regardless of colour, culture, medical conditions, gender, sexuality, or anything else. We share this same starting point with every other person without exception. This is a beautiful perspective on humanity and it is helpful to humanity. This is what we should expect if God is real, and God is love. This is yet another reason why Christianity is beautiful.

A BEAUTIFUL PEOPLE (KNOWN AS THE CHURCH)?

If Christianity is compelling, should we not expect the Christian Church to be compelling also? If the good and loving God proclaimed by Christianity is real, then would we not expect beauty and not ugliness in the Church? So, is it beautiful?

Some would say no. Churches can be marked by politics within, and the politicking gets nasty. Church people can also be known for politicking beyond the church, and that can be brutal also. Plus, the Christian Church appears to be greatly divided. Not only are there many different camps, there are even different camps within the camps! This can all seem quite ugly to the onlooker.

While there is ugliness, is there also beauty? Do the writings of the Bible point to a compelling and beautiful vision for the Church? There is so much we could say, but let us take the words of Jesus in John 14 as a starting point.

> *"I tell you the truth, anyone who believes in me will do the same works I have done, and even greater works, because I am going to be with the Father. John 14:12 (NLT)*

The Christian Church is to be a people who do great works. We may be startled by the idea that Christians could do "greater works" than Jesus. Perhaps we immediately think of miraculous works of great power and wonder how anyone could ever match Jesus' healing ministry. However, we should note that Jesus' greatest work was not a health-restoring miracle, but His relationship-restoring death and resurrection. While reconciliation to God is something only God can accomplish, the Church is called to participate in God's work of reconciliation! Consider the words of Paul,

> And all of this is a gift from God, who brought us back to himself through Christ. **And God has given us this task of reconciling people to him**. For God was in Christ, reconciling the world to himself, no longer counting people's sins against them. **And he gave us this wonderful message of reconciliation. So we are Christ's ambassadors; God is making his appeal through us.** We speak for Christ when we plead, "Come back to God!" For God made Christ, who never sinned, to be the offering for our sin, so that we could be made right with God through Christ. 2 Corinthians 5:18-21 (NLT emphasis added)

The Christian Church has been involved in this ministry of reconciliation throughout the world over the past 2000 years or so. This is a great work, and it is beautiful.

We can go on to speak of the many other good works that Christians have been involved in. Alvin Schmidt outlines the positive impact of the Christian Church on the world in his book, "How Christianity Changed the World[7]." Consider his chapter titles as an indication of that impact:

1. People Transformed by Jesus Christ
2. The Sanctification of Human Life
3. Christianity Elevates Sexual Morality
4. Women Receive Freedom and Dignity
5. Charity and Compassion: Their Christian Connection
6. Hospitals and Health Care: Their Christian Roots
7. Christianity's Imprint on Education
8. Labor and Economic Freedom Dignified
9. Science: Its Christian Connections
10. Liberty and Justice for All
11. Slavery Abolished: A Christian Achievement
12. Christianity's Stamp on Art and Architecture
13. The Sound of Music: Its Christian Resonance
14. Hallmarks of Literature: Their Christian Imprint
15. Additional influence: Holidays, Words, Symbols and Expressions

The positive impact of the Christian Church on the world has been massive and beautiful. I encourage you to read Alvin's book to discover just how massive and beautiful it has been. Yes, Christians have often got it wrong and brought ugliness and not beauty. But over the centuries, God has used His people for beautiful purposes. Good

---

[7] Alvin J. Schmidt, How Christianity Changed the World. Zondervan, 2009. (Kindle)

things have happened and keep happening through the people known as the Church.

Let us consider the next two verses of John 14:

> *You can ask for anything in my name, and I will do it, so that the Son can bring glory to the Father. Yes, ask me for anything in my name, and I will do it! John 14:13-14 (NLT)*

The Christian Church is to be a people who ask in Jesus' name. To ask 'in his name' means that we are to be a people who rally around his purposes. These verses do not indicate that Jesus will bend to our will, something we might desire as we consider what amazing-in-our-eyes things we might include under "anything." Rather, in asking 'in Jesus' name', Jesus' will is becoming ours. We begin to see what is amazing in His eyes.

Most Sunday mornings I choose a tie to go with a shirt. Most Sunday mornings my wife will say something like "you are not going out dressed like that, are you?" I might try to bend my wife's will to accept my clothing choice, but it never goes that way. It is not that my wife wins a battle of wills. It is that I am steered in a better direction. I am not upset with being called out on my tie selections. I am very pleased to be better dressed! When all is said and done I realise that my ultimate desire was not to wear a particular tie with a particular shirt anyway, but to be well dressed.

This is like our relationship with God. It is not that God wins the battle of wills and we should be grumpy about that. It is that we are steered in a better direction and we can be thrilled about that. When all is said and done we realise that what God has for us is really what we would have wanted all along and would have asked for if our eyes had been open to all the possibilities.

The Christian Church is a people who are steered by God, who pray in Jesus' name, seeking His Kingdom, not our empires, and His purposes, not our flights of fancy. This is beautiful!

Let us consider the next verse:

> *"If you love me, obey my commandments. John 14:15 (NLT)*

The Christian Church is a people who love Jesus, who have an allegiance to Jesus.

We are to be a people who put the teaching of Jesus into practice. We are to love our neighbours, and love our enemies. We are to grow in character. We are to make disciples. It is beautiful when a person lives out the teaching of Jesus.

We are to be a people who emulate Jesus. We seek to reflect the goodness of Jesus in the way we relate to people and are relatable. We do good. We live grace-filled lives, ready to forgive. The Christian Church is to be a Jesusemulating people. It is beautiful when a person emulates Jesus.

Let us consider the next few verses:

> *And I will ask the Father, and he will give you another Advocate, who will never leave you. He is the Holy Spirit, who leads into all truth. The world cannot receive him, because it isn't looking for him and doesn't recognize him. But you know him, because he lives with you now and later will be in you. John 14:16-17 (NLT)*

The Christian Church is to be a people who are impacted by the Holy Spirit. This means a number of things including the fact that we are being transformed by the Spirit:

> *But the Holy Spirit produces this kind of fruit in our lives: love, joy, peace, patience, kindness, goodness, faithfulness, gentleness, and self-control. There is no law against these things! . . . Since we are living by the Spirit, let us follow the Spirit's leading in every part of our lives. Galatians 5:22-23,25 (NLT)*

It is a beautiful thing when people are transformed by the Spirit!

Conclusion.

The Church can sometimes be quite ugly, however, the Biblical vision for the Church is beautiful. The Church is to be a people wrapped up in a deep life-changing connection with the Divine. When church is ugly, there is always a disconnect from God. When there is connection, the Church is truly beautiful; a people involved in God's great works, a people who pray in Jesus' name and rally around his purposes, a people who have an allegiance to Jesus, a people filled with, and led by, the Holy Spirit. The Biblical vision for the Church is consistent with what you would expect from a good and loving God. The beauty of the Church in that vision is another aspect of Christianity that is compelling.

A BEAUTIFUL VISION OF THE FUTURE?

Does Christianity have a beautiful vision for the future? It would be odd if you were considering the reasons to be a Christian, but then upon asking about the afterlife you are told that you enter an endless cycle of being reincarnated as a bird if you trust Jesus, and as a worm, if not. That should strike you as nonsense. Now what about Christian teaching? The idea that upon death we either sprout wings and play a harp while sitting in the clouds, or burn in an eternal fire, is for many people, too much to believe. It is for me too!

Is the Christian vision for the future we find in the Biblical writings consistent with a good and loving God? Or is it nonsensical? When we hear what the Bible teaches about our eternal destination, do we say 'Of course, that is what a good God would do"?

Let us look first, to the Book of Revelation;

> *Then I saw a new heaven and a new earth; for the first heaven and the first earth had passed away, and the sea was no more. (Revelation 21:1)*

Here we have, not a hope of going up into heaven when I die, to spend eternity there, but something much grander. This is a vision of God's re-creation of all creation. All of creation has been negatively impacted by the sin of humanity[8]. All of creation will be positively impacted by God's rescue of humanity.

> *And I saw the holy city, the new Jerusalem, coming down out of heaven from God, prepared as a bride adorned for her husband. (Revelation 21:2)*

Here we are told of a city, not in the sense of roads and buildings, but in the sense of people. The holy city is the "bride," that is, the people of God. Just as people are the focus in the creation account of Genesis, people are the focus of the re-creation account. God created humanity, the only creature we are told are created in the image of the Divine, for a special relationship. That relationship is what is truly important:

> *And I heard a loud voice from the throne saying,*
> *"See, the home of God is among mortals.*
> *He will dwell with them;*
> *they will be his peoples,*
> *and God himself will be with them; (Revelation 21:3)*

There is much in the Bible about separation from God being a huge problem for humanity. It begins with Genesis chapter three and the banishment of Adam and Eve from

---

[8] see Romans 8:18-23

the Garden of Eden. It becomes apparent at Mount Sinai when the people cannot approach the mountain on which God's presence was made palpable. It is emphasised in the books of Exodus, Leviticus, and Numbers, with the establishment of both the tabernacle and priesthood. While God was willing to dwell among his people, as symbolised through the pitching of his "tent" among them, God needed to remain separated from the people, for their sake. An unholy people cannot approach a holy God without becoming holy first. The sacrificial rigmarole of the priesthood was a constant reminder of separation from God and the need for "atonement" or as some people say it, "at-one-ment." The priesthood and the sacrifices spoken of in the Old Testament books point forward to something greater; God came to us in Jesus. We killed him. He offers forgiveness anyway. In Jesus the future of God's people is wrapped up with being at home with the Divine, with God who loves and forgives. There is no more separation from God.

The problems of this world, which separation from God creates, also are dealt with;

> *he will wipe every tear from their eyes.*
> **Death will be no more;**
> *mourning and crying and pain will be no more,*
> *for the first things have passed away." Revelation 21:4*
> *(NRSV emphasis added)*

The consequence of separation from God is death. The consequence of being reconciled to God is eternal life. In

Jesus, death is no longer our final destination. The consequence of God's grace is not just eternal life; as we have already seen, it is eternal life *with God* which is infinitely better.

In summary, the Biblical vision of the future is one of transformation, for all creation, for our bodies, and for our very selves. The transformation within us begins now through the Holy Spirit. The fact that the Christian can look to God to restore everything in the future is beautiful. The fact that the Christian need not wait for Christ's return to begin that good work in us is also beautiful. The hope of meaningful change, not into brilliant cloud-sitting harpists, but into good people who dwell with a good God in a good creation, is consistent with a good and loving God.

However, is the future of those who completely reject God consistent with a good and loving God? The idea of someone being in a fire forever because they don't believe in Jesus does not seem consistent to many of us. In thinking about this we must first appreciate that the people who wrote the Scriptures often thought in poetic ways, just as we do today. We sometimes pick apart the Bible as if we are in math class working out equations. Let us remember our English literature lessons and have an appreciation for the poetic and literary nuances which can escape the math whizzes. We will not dig into this too deeply, but it is best to take the language about hell, with the everlasting fire and torment, as poetic. The least poetic, the most matter-of-fact, the most precise and concise description of hell we have in the Bible is this;

What is hell? It is separation from God. What is it like to be separated from God? Thankfully, no one alive can truly tell, for to be alive at all is to experience a measure of God's grace and presence. However, we do well to remember that "the wages of sin is death, but the free gift of God is eternal life in Christ Jesus our Lord"[9]. As you read through the Bible, watch out for how often salvation is spoken of as a matter of eternal life versus death. This is consistent with the Genesis account and the promise that death would occur if the forbidden fruit were eaten. What we can say with certainty is that to experience hell is to experience everlasting separation from God. I, and many others, think this means to cease to experience any kind of life at all.

If hell is separation from God, then is separation from God consistent with a good and loving God? Consider first, the holiness and justice of God. That unholy people cannot dwell with a holy God is made clear in Exodus, Leviticus, and Numbers; at Mount Sinai, and through the establishment of the tabernacle and priesthood. God did not allow for teaching about His holiness and our sinfulness in the Old Testament, then come to us in the New Testament and say "it doesn't matter anymore." It does matter, but God offers to make us holy in Jesus and through

---

[9] Romans 6:23 NRSV

his Holy Spirit. If you reject God fully completely, then separation from God is a very natural consequence. The experience of death is a natural consequence of refusing the offer of life from the Life-Giver. Therefore, the future of those who reject God is consistent with a good and loving God who respects the wishes of those who want nothing to do with him. Of course that is what a good God would do.

The Biblical writings present a compelling and beautiful vision for the future of those who desire a relationship with God. While we might not use the word beautiful, the vision of the future of those who do not want a relationship with God is consistent with His goodness and love. The consistency of the Christian vision of the future is beautiful.

PART 2

IS CHRISTIANITY BELIEVABLE?

"Don't go to Bible College." That was the advice given to me by a member of our Baptist "credentials committee" when I sat before them as a nineteen year old who felt a tug to become a pastor. Instead I should go to a secular university and be sure to take some psychology and philosophy. So I did. It was during my time at Trent University that I came to a conclusion that has affected the shape of my faith and given me direction in with regard to spirituality and life. While I *felt* great assurance of God's love in Jesus, if this "Christianity thing" were true, *it should also make sense*. It would be reasonable. It should be believable.

Can we really believe what was written in the Bible so long ago? With so many world-views, and so many religions, how could we ever pick just one? Hasn't science kicked all religious views to the curb? Does it really matter what you believe, so long as you are sincere, and don't bother others with it? Don't people need to leave their brains at the door of a Christian church? Let us review why Christianity is believable, why one need neither leave their brain at the door of the church, nor their faith in the university parking lot.

BELIEVABLE TRUTH?

How can we know if anything is true?. If we can't know anything to be true, how can we ever be sure Christianity is true? If Christianity is not true, it is truly not compelling.

The idea of truth permeates the arrest of Jesus in the Gospel of John, chapter 18. Jesus appealed to truth, then Peter denied the truth, then the religious leaders lied, then Pilate tried to get to the truth. This was all capped off with the following:

> *Pilate said, "So you are a king?"*
> *Jesus responded, "You say I am a king. Actually, I was born and came into the world to testify to the truth. All who love the truth recognize that what I say is true."*
> *"What is truth?" Pilate asked. John 18:37-38 (NLT)*

What was Pilate's tone of voice when he asked "what is truth?" If you were an actor how would you portray it? Would you portray Pilate as a philosopher on a quest for knowledge? "Hmmm, an interesting question I would love to spend some time pondering though I doubt we can ever know." Or would you portray Pilate as a busy man who wanted to get back to his own plans for the day? "What does your version of truth matter when I've got so much more to worry about?!"

These represent two approaches to truth today. There are those who get all philosophical about truth and say, "We cannot be sure of anything, so don't tell me about Jesus." Then there are those who just don't care; "It just doesn't matter, we've got more important things to think about, so don't tell me about Jesus." Let us look at both.

Can we know the truth?

How do we know that the entirety of our lives is not just some big dream and we will wake up some day to find that we actually exist in an entirely different world? How do we know we are not kept alive by machines or aliens in a state of dreaming as in the Matrix movies? Can we be 100% sure Christianity is true if we cannot be 100% sure anything is true? Can we be certain beyond all possible doubt?

Here's the thing; we do not live as as if we cannot know anything. We live as people who know stuff! We are never 100% sure of anything before we make decisions. Pilate, after he asked, "what is truth?", immediately went to the people to report what he knew to be true:

> *"What is truth?" Pilate asked. Then he went out again to the people and told them, "He is not guilty of any crime." John 18:38 (NLT)*

Pilate had enough certainty to be able to form an opinion and make a decision. *This is how we live.*

I had a scary experience many years ago. The roads were icy and I lost control of my car causing me to be on the wrong side of the road. I did not take the time to ponder if it was all a dream, or that possibly the truck bearing down on me was just a hallucination. After all, anything is possible. Rather, I knew I was in trouble, I made the right decisions and got the car under control again. This is how we live, not knowing things to be true beyond *all* possible doubt, but beyond a *reasonable* doubt. We make decisions all the time, not because we can be 100% certain we are correct, but because it is reasonable to think that we may be correct.

But don't extraordinary claims, such as "Jesus is Lord," or "Jesus is alive," require extraordinary evidence, as people sometimes claim? Consider that in the first century ordinary people experienced the extraordinary person of Jesus in ordinary ways. They could be as sure about him as I could be sure about my situation in a skidding car. With the exception of Paul and his Damascus road experience, those who experienced Jesus experienced him in the same way they would experience anyone. This was true before Easter, when ordinary people heard his extraordinary teaching and witnessed his extraordinary miracles in ordinary ways. This was also true following Easter when people saw Jesus alive again. Yes, he was even more extraordinary than before, but again, ordinary people were experiencing his extraordinary presence in normal ways. They were not having visions or dreams, they were experiencing life, they were experiencing a very real Jesus in front of them. They could see him and touch him. They knew him to be real, just as they would know anything to be real:

We proclaim to you the one who existed from the beginning, whom we have heard and seen. We saw him with our own eyes and touched him with our own hands. He is the Word of life. This one who is life itself was revealed to us, and we have seen him. And now we testify and proclaim to you that he is the one who is eternal life. He was with the Father, and then he was revealed to us. We proclaim to you what we ourselves have actually seen and heard so that you may have fellowship with us. And our fellowship is with the Father and with his Son, Jesus Christ. We are writing these things so that you may fully share our joy. 1 John 1:1-4 (NLT)

All those who saw Jesus risen from the dead were ordinary people experiencing the extraordinary person of Jesus in ordinary ways. They could be as sure of him as they could be sure of anything.

Now we could say "it is possible that the risen Jesus was actually an alien imposter," for anything is possible. But we don't live that way. Neither did people in the first century. They knew beyond a reasonable doubt that this was Jesus, now alive, though once dead. The question is not whether the claims of Christianity are true beyond all *possible* doubt, but if they are true beyond a *reasonable* doubt. We will be looking at some reasons to think so in the chapters that follow.

So can we know anything? Yes, we reasonably know things to be true. However, does it matter?

Does truth matter?

We live as if truth matters - a lot. Back to my scary experience in the car. I knew that moment could have changed my life for the rest of my days, if I had any more days left in this life. Reality matters! What is true with respect to Jesus matters incredibly. Grasping the reality of Jesus is not the same as forming an opinion on whether Coke is a better cola than Pepsi, or whether the Boston Bruins are a better team than the Toronto Maple Leafs. It is more like grasping the reality of a truck bearing down on you. It impacts every moment of your future. Why do people often live as if truth matters, but when it comes to spiritual things, it suddenly does not? It matters more! Truth matters - a lot. Spiritual truths matter a lot more.

Why has truth been challenged in our day?

Deceit and deception are at the heart of "the Fall" as described in Genesis chapter 3. Adam and Eve were deceived. Sinking into that deception they sinned, creating a wedge between themselves and God. There are deceptions today which keep that wedge in place.

Deceit and deception ran through the trial and crucifixion of Jesus. The ones who wanted Jesus dead attempted to deceive Pilate who was not totally deceived by them, knowing that Jesus was innocent of their accusations. However, Pilate failed to recognise that the deception mattered. He thought his relationship with the people under his charge was more important than his relationship with the one now under his judgement, the One under whose charge he himself was.

Ironically, while the crucifixion of Jesus happened because of failure to apprehend the truth, it is a clear window into the truth, that,

> ....*God is love. God showed how much he loved us by sending his one and only Son into the world so that we might have eternal life through him. This is real love—not that we loved God, but that he loved us and sent his Son as a sacrifice to take away our sins. 1 John 4:8-10 (NLT)*

Deception ran through the Fall. Deception ran through the trial and crucifixion of Jesus. Will we let deception run through our lives? God is love. That is a truth which can be known and which matters more than anything!

A BELIEVABLE ACCOUNT OF THE COSMOS?

The heavens declare the glory of God; the skies proclaim the work of his hands. Psalm 19:1 (NIV)

You can imagine the writer in Psalm 19 looking up to the stars in awe, praising God for all creation. But do the heavens still declare the glory of God in our day? Do the skies still proclaim the work of his hands to a people as sophisticated and knowledgeable as we are? The heavens would compel the ancients to glorify God as Creator. But with all we now know about cosmology through science, are we compelled to worship in our day?

It turns out that the heavens still speak. Philosophers and scientists do the talking[10], but through the study of "the heavens," what we call the cosmos, we can learn something about the existence and nature of God.

Let us look to three questions inspired by the heavens.

First question; what caused the beginning of the universe?

---

[10] Author and podcaster Frank Turek has stated that science doesn't say anything but scientists do.

Beginning in the last century, many scientists were won over to the view that our universe had a beginning. While some Christians balked at the "Big Bang" theory, others saw the implications for theology. After all, people of the Judeo-Christian tradition have long been saying that the universe had a beginning. William Lane Craig[11] lays out what he calls the Kalam Cosmological argument in this way:

1. Whatever begins to exist has a cause.
2. The universe began to exist.
3. Therefore, the universe has a cause.

Since scientists have been telling us that the universe had a beginning at some point, there must be some reason it came into existence. A Creator God is one possibility!

Further, Craig argues that the cause must be spaceless, timeless, immaterial, uncaused, and powerful. Sound like anyone you know? God, as revealed in the Biblical Scriptures, fits this cause of the universe perfectly. But then we might object with "who created God?" Consider the first premise above, and then note that God does not begin to exist, therefore we do not need to consider what caused his existence.[12]

Second question; Why are the conditions just right at the beginning of the universe for it to be life permitting?

---

[11] See William Lane Craig's resources as listed in "For Further Reading".

[12] For a concise video from William Lane Craig on the Kalam Cosmological argument, please visit https://youtu.be/6CulBuMCLgO

Scientists tell us that certain physical constants, like the force of gravity, are so very specific, that if they were just slightly different at the beginning, the universe would not exist as we know it. It would not be life permitting. This is commonly called the Fine Tuning Argument.

Just how specific must these constants be? Dr. Hugh Ross in his book, The Creator and the Cosmos[13], comments on one such constant, the ratio of electrons to protons:

> One part in 10^{37} is such an incredibly sensitive balance that it is hard to visualize. The following analogy might help: Cover the entire North American continent in dimes all the way up to the moon, a height of about 239,000 miles . . . Next, pile dimes from here to the moon on a billion other continents the same size as North America. Paint one dime red and mix it into the billions of piles of dimes. Blindfold a friend and ask him to pick out one dime. The odds that he will pick the red dime are one in 10^{37}.

Did this degree of fine tuning happen by necessity, chance, or by design? Design can be shown to be the most reasonable alternative. We are only scratching the surface

---

[13] Hugh Ross, The Creator and the Cosmos: How the Latest Scientific Discoveries Reveal God. Reasons to Believe, 2018 (Kindle Edition)

here, I encourage you to dig more deeply, William Lane Craig's works being very helpful here.[14]

Third question; Why does anything exist at all?

Looking up to the heavens above on a starry night, we might ask why is there anything at all? Gottfried Leibniz put it: "why is there something rather than nothing?". He then went on to show how God is the answer. William Lane Craig has formulated Leibniz's thinking using the following premises[15]:

1. Everything that exists has an explanation of its existence (either in the necessity of its own nature or in an external cause).
2. If the universe has an explanation of its existence, that explanation is God.
3. The universe exists.
4. The explanation of the universe's existence is God.

This can be a tricky one to wrap our minds around, but basically the idea is that the universe is contingent, that is, something else was required for its existence. We experience this in daily life as we recognise that all things have some cause behind them. There is a computer here in

---

[14] Please see the works of William Lane Craig as listed in "For Further Reading," but especially helpful is the short video found at https://youtu.be/EE76nwimuTO

[15] Please see the works of William Lane Craig as listed in "For Further Reading".

front of me because someone built it, and I bought it. This computer did not need to exist, nor did I have to buy it. Its existence and placement is contingent on many things. However, God exists necessarily. One could argue that only God would exist necessarily. Nothing caused God to exist. The only way a contingent universe could exist is if something which existed necessarily caused it to exist. This is consistent with what the Bible teaches.[16]

In Summary,

As we look to the cosmos, we discover that what was written so long ago in the Christian Scriptures is consistent with what is being learned through science and philosophy in our day. Thus far, Christianity is believable.

---

[16] For a short video by William Lane Craig which explains the Leibniz argument much better than I can please visit https://youtu.be/FPCzEPOoD7I

A BELIEVABLE ACCOUNT OF MORALITY?

Are Christians better than everyone else? Are they more moral? Are they more likely to do the right thing, the good thing? Are people compelled to believe in God because Christians are moral people? If so, perhaps we could say the morality of Christians demonstrates that Christianity is believable. Unfortunately, Christians can be immoral, and fortunately, non-Christians can be moral. So this chapter should be over, right?

The moral performance of Christians may not be compelling as evidence that Christianity is believable, but the fact of morality itself is. The very fact that everyone can point to immoral Christians and moral non-Christians points to the existence of God. How so? Let's take a look.

In the previous chapter we considered Psalm 19 and how the universe points to the existence of God. Some Bible scholars believe that Psalm 19 is actually two Psalms because there is a sudden shift following verse 6 from speaking of planetary systems to speaking of morality:

> *In the heavens he has set a tent for the sun,*
> *which comes out like a bridegroom from his wedding*
> *canopy,*
> *and like a strong man runs its course with joy.*
> *Its rising is from the end of the heavens,*
> *and its circuit to the end of them;*
> *and nothing is hid from its heat.*
> ***The law of the Lord is perfect,***
> ***reviving the soul;***
> ***the decrees of the Lord are sure,***
> ***making wise the simple;***
> ***the precepts of the Lord are right,***
> ***rejoicing the heart;***
> ***the commandment of the Lord is clear,***
> ***enlightening the eyes****; Psalms 19:4-8 (NRSV emphasis*
> *added to point out the shift from speaking of the cosmos*
> *to morality)*

While we might see a change in subject from cosmology to morality here making us think this was originally two Psalms, is this really a big shift? We read about the sun following its course in verses 4-6. Though written, of course, from the perspective of the Psalmist standing on earth, we know from scientific discoveries that the planets and the sun are following the laws of physics. God created these laws so there could be a well-functioning, life-permitting-and-sustaining universe. Verse 7 then turns to another kind of law which is given by God for a well-functioning, life-permitting-and-sustaining universe; the moral law. When the sun and the planets follow God's laws of physics, life works well for everyone. When people follow God's laws for morality, life works well for everyone.

Imagine for a moment what would happen if the sun and earth did not follow the laws of physics. It would be catastrophic. We do not get very far into the Bible before we discover what happens when people do not follow the moral law. Had Cain kept to God's moral law, it would have gone so much better for Abel. It would have gone so much better for Adam and Eve. It would have gone so much better for Cain also, Abel's brother and murderer.

Experience confirms what the Bible teaches; life just does not work well without morals. The vast majority of people know that morals are important and good for the well being of humanity, even if they do not like certain ones. The Psalmist knows that the laws of physics point to a Creator. The laws of morality do also. As Psalm 19 points out, both are part of God's life sustaining universe.

Philosophy confirms that there is a moral lawgiver. If we say there is no God, then we can not speak of objective morals existing either. You might disagree. After all, don't different cultures have different moral standards? Do you think, however, that there are certain things which would be wrong for all people in every place and time? Is murder on a whim ever okay? Most of us would think not. Either objective morality exists, or morals are just subjective and are determined by social norms and personal preference. Either murder on a whim is truly wrong, or we just prefer it not happen so that society can function well. When ancient peoples conducted the practice of "exposing" a child, that is, leaving an unwanted infant to die, was that wrong? If God does not exist, if there is no lawgiver, then it was not objectively wrong. Some atheists are willing to suggest that morality is subjective, a matter of preference from society to society, but not too many people go that far. If human rights are real, then so too are objective morals, and then so too is God.[17]

Are Christians better than everyone else? Perhaps not. There are atheists who live very moral lives, and there are Christians who live very immoral lives. However, the very fact we can point that out is evidence that objective morality is real. It is therefore evidence that God is real. If you find the existence of objective morals believable, then you can find the existence of God to be believable also.

---

[17] To learn more about what is called the "moral argument for the existence of God", please see the works cited in "For Further Reading". For a short video that describes this better than I can, please go to https://youtu.be/OxiAikEk2vU

A BELIEVABLE ACCOUNT OF LIFE?

Why is there life? It turns out there are a number of further questions worthy of consideration.

First, how did the earth become suitable for life? Despite the longing for "life out there", many scientists tell us the odds are against life happening anywhere, even here! Many things need to come together with precision for life to be possible. They happen to do so for us here on planet earth. The earth just happens to have the right qualities such as the right atmosphere, right orbit, right tilt (thanks moon!), right weather patterns, right core temperature, right distance from, and right orbit around, the right kind of sun which is in the right place in our galaxy. We are only scratching the surface of things that need to come together for life to be possible. The earth appears to be a finely calibrated machine for the flourishing of life. When we see such precision in any other machine we don't normally ask "How did that happen?", we ask "Who did that?".

Second, how did life come about in the first place? Why is the universe not made up solely of non-living matter? In the past we were taught that life began with very simple organisms in a "primordial soup. " However, life is incredibly complex even in its simplest expressions. The simplest of life forms require complex machinery and teamwork among

the parts. I don't know why but as a student in school I
used to take my pens apart and write with just the ink tube
and the attached ball-point. The pen could be reduced to
very few parts and still work. Living things, however, cannot
be reduced like that. They are more like a mechanical watch
where messing with one cog renders the watch useless.
Living things are way more complex. When we see complex
machinery working well we don't ask "How did that
happen?", we ask "Who did that?".

Also, life happens thanks to an incredible amount of
information such as we find in DNA. How did all that
information get there? When I was a youth anytime I saw a
Commodore 64 computer on display in a store, I wrote a
short program that would write the same words over and
over again on the screen. I knew just enough of the
computer language called "Basic" to be able to do that. I
am sure no K-Mart employee on finding the computer would
have asked, "How did that happen?". Rather, they would ask
the obvious question, "Who wrote that?".

**Third, How did there come to be incredible diversity and
inter-dependance among amazing living things?** If life
came about simply by chance why is the world not just
covered in something like moss? Why such wonderful, often
beautiful and awe-inspiring living things which depend on
the existence of other beautiful and awe inspiring forms of
life? How did eco-systems come about which require the
very diversity found within them? Living things are found in
environments where not only can they themselves flourish,

but importantly, they are necessary for the flourishing of other living things in the environment also.

We are very often told that animals "adapted" to their environments. However, did they adapt against the odds, or were they, plus their environments, adapted to each other by design? When we see race cars whizzing around race tracks do we wonder how the cars adapted and became so fast? When we see trucks hauling heavy loads down a highway, do we ask how they adapted, becoming so big? We can speak of the evolution of the vehicle, but we know that intelligence is behind that evolution. It is believable that adaptation of things to environments is a matter of design, a matter of creation. When we see things uniquely placed according to what they are we do not ask "How did that happen?", we ask "Who did that?".

The real question.

John Entwistle, bass player for "The Who," released a solo project including a song called "I Wonder" in which he marvelled at the way things were put together[18]. The song includes these lines in the chorus:

> *Thank you Mother Nature*
> *For the way you got things planned*
> *Don't ever change a thing, I'm happy as I am.*

---

[18] You can listen to the song at https://youtu.be/OX4tlwT5Xss

In thinking about nature perhaps he was on the right track. There is a "who?" behind the "what?" and the "how?" questions.

The precise alignment of parameters required for life to flourish on earth points to intelligence and capability. The complexity found within even the simplest of living things points to intelligence and capability. The use of language in the building blocks of life points to intelligence and capability. The care shown through the placement of living things in finely balanced eco-systems points to intelligence and capability. The question is not "how," but "who?". Who has this kind of intelligence and capability?

Christianity provides a believable answer to the question; "who?". Consider what we discover in response to the questions posed above in the first two chapters of Genesis:

1. On the suitability of the earth for life, God put all the necessary conditions and circumstances into place for life. Obvious things are mentioned like light, dark, the sun, the moon, water and land[19]. We are not told about things like gravity, oxygen, and the like. We should not expect a science report from a writing that is introducing us to God! Nor should we treat the Bible like a science report.

2. On life getting started in the first place, God, a living being, created life and living things. In being created

---

[19] see Genesis 1:1-19.

and designed by God, living things are complex right
from the start. In fact living things are created
with "seed in it"[20], that is, the ability to reproduce is
baked right in. How could non-living, non-thinking, non-
creating things give rise to living, thinking things
capable of reproduction?

3. On diverse living things being found in well balanced
    eco-systems, God created life according to their kinds[21].
    Food is provided[22]. The required systems are put in
    place for life to flourish.

As we consider life and living things, there is one more
question.

**Why do human beings seem to be different from all other
living things in remarkable ways?** There is a difference in
intelligence, creativity, language skills, morality, and
religion. There is an ability to reflect and a desire for
significance that does not seem to be found in other living
things.

When a child in an orphanage is taken into a family where
they are then fed, clothed, coached, taught, and experience
loving and caring relationship for many, many years, we do
not ask "how did that happen?". When we see a child cared

---

[20] Genesis 1:11.

[21] see Genesis 1:20-25.

[22] see Genesis 1:29-31.

for in such remarkable ways, we ask, "who desired a special relationship with that child?".

Back to Genesis chapters one and two. God created humanity in His image, and for a special relationship. Biblical scholars point to two accounts of creation, the first being found in chapter one and the second being found in chapter two. In the first account humanity is created last, but "in his image"[23]. The second account has humanity created first[24]. Both accounts point to how we were created by God for a special relationship.

The life, teaching, miracles, death, and resurrection of Jesus are also a confirmation that God has created us for a special relationship. God did something special for humanity about 2000 years ago in Jesus. Why? Because humanity has had a special place in God's heart from the beginning. Humans are different from all other living things because we were created for a special relationship. If God does not exist, then how does one account for how different humans are from other living things?

In Summary.

What the Biblical writings tell us about God, our creator and redeemer, fits very well with the questions raised about life through philosophy and science. When we consider these questions of life and living things, it turns out there is a

---

[23] see Genesis 1:26.

[24] see Genesis 2:4-9.

more compelling question than "how?". It is "Who?". "God" is a believable and good answer. Here is another way in which Christianity is believable.

A BELIEVABLE ACCOUNT OF THE MIND?

If you are reading this book, then hopefully you are engaged in thought! Does our ability to think point to the existence of God?

Christianity gives a good account for the reason we can freely think for ourselves. If there is nothing supernatural, if there is only matter and the physical, then the brain operates just like a machine, and therefore potentially none of our thinking is free thinking. Rather, our thoughts are like the falling of dominoes. Or, to use another example, they are like the weather. We might experience a "random" gust of wind. However, a gust of wind is never random. The air is simply following the laws of physics and under the circumstances, the gust had to blow the way it did. If there is no God, then the same may be true of our thinking. Every thought, though seemingly random, had to happen as it did. If this is the case, how can we hold people accountable for anything?

However, we intuitively know that we have free-will. Christianity accounts for this experience of freewill. Our minds are more than mere machines.

Christianity gives a good account for the reason we can reason in the first place. How do we get from a brain to a mind? How do we get from physical matter to conscious thought? The brain and the mind interact, but they are different.

Lee Strobel, in his book "The Case for the Creator"[25] gives the example from Sam Parnia of the brain being like a television. The television is necessary for the watching of a movie or show, but the signal carrying the show is quite a separate thing. Should the television be damaged, it will be hard for the signal to get through properly, but the signal is still a separate entity. So too with our brains. A physical problem with the brain will affect how the mind is expressed, yet they are not one and the same thing. In fact, there is no good theory as to how the two work together.

How did the brain give rise to consciousness in the first place? Strobel goes on to quote J.P. Moreland on this question:

> *Here's the point: you can't get something from nothing . . . It's as simple as that. If there were no God, then the history of the entire universe, up until the appearance of living creatures, would be a history of dead matter with no consciousness. You would not have any thoughts, beliefs, feelings, sensations, free actions, choices, or purposes. There would be simply*

---

[25] Lee Strobel, The Case for a Creator. A Journalist Investigates Scientific Evidence That Points Toward God. Zondervan, 2005.

one physical event after another physical event, behaving according to the laws of physics and chemistry. . . . How, then, do you get something totally different – conscious, living, thinking, feeling, believing creatures – from materials that don't have that? That's getting something from nothing! And that's the main problem.

However, there is no problem accounting for the rise of consciousness in the Christian worldview. Continuing to quote Moreland:

. . . .you see, the Christian worldview begins with thought and feeling and belief and desire and choice. That is, God is conscious. God has thoughts. He has beliefs, he has desires, he has awareness, he's alive, he acts with purpose. We start there. And because we start with the mind of God, we don't have a problem with explaining the origin of our mind.

Strobel also references Phillip Johnson: "you either have 'in the beginning were the particles,' or 'in the beginning was the Logos,' which means 'divine mind.'" Logos is often translated as "word" in the Bible, for example;

In the beginning was the Word, and the Word was with God, and the Word was God. He was with God in the beginning. Through him all things were made; without him nothing was made that has been made. John 1:1-3 (NIV)

When we consider the evidence of consciousness and free minds we can infer an intelligent, conscious and free agent, we can infer the existence of a Creator. Christianity fits that inference very well. Our minds are yet another facet of Christianity that is believable. Thinking points to the One Who thought us up in the first place!

A BELIEVABLE ACCOUNT OF RELIGION?

Religion often gets a bad rap. From the infamous saying by Christopher Hitchens "religion poisons everything," to my own disdain for religion and anything religious. Yes, I am a Baptist pastor, and yes, I sometimes agree with Christopher Hitchens that religion can poison everything! Religion has destroyed many lives. May the Lord forgive me for any time I have spoken poison into the lives of others in the name of religion.

However, when it comes to the topic of religion, Christianity provides a believable account for why there is religion in the first place. While walking through Athens, Paul was both impressed and disturbed by the amount of religious devotion he saw:

> *While Paul was waiting for them in Athens, he was greatly distressed to see that the city was full of idols. . . .Paul then stood up in the meeting of the Areopagus and said: "People of Athens! I see that in every way you are very religious. For as I walked around and looked carefully at your objects of worship, I even found an altar with this inscription: to an unknown god. So you are ignorant of the very thing*

you worship—and this is what I am going to proclaim to you. Acts 16,17:22-23 NIV

Walking through Athens is much like taking a walk through all the world throughout history; religion and the expression of spirituality has been the default for humanity. There is a religious impulse, a desire, a reaching to grasp hold of something greater than ourselves. You might think otherwise if you are a Westerner, but even here in secular Canada, spiritualities and religions are still very popular despite an education that is very much slanted toward scientism.

Why is there such a religious impulse among people? Why do we seem to be different from other living things in this respect? C.S. Lewis, in his book "Mere Christianity,"[26] points out that we have desires that correspond to things that exist. So, for example, we desire food, and food exists. We desire sex, and there is such a thing as sex. So too with our spiritual longings. Our longings for something greater than ourselves point to something, or Someone greater than ourselves. If we evolved from a purely natural process and there is no God, then why do we have any spiritual inclination at all? Christianity provides a reason as to why religion exists; because God exists and He created us for relationship with Him. The yearnings for a higher power point to the reality of God.

---

[26] Lewis, C.S. Mere Christianity. (Kindle)

A BELIEVABLE EXPLANATION OF EVIL?

If the Biblical writers are correct about God, that God is, and God is love, then why is the world in a mess? Why is there suffering?

Yes, the Bible tells us that God is love, but the Bible also points out that the world is in a mess. First off, notice that humanity's relationship with God is destroyed by sin right there in the opening chapters of Genesis. Adam and Eve were free to enjoy the Garden of Eden, except that there was one thing they ought not do:

> *"You may freely eat the fruit of every tree in the garden— except the tree of the knowledge of good and evil. If you eat its fruit, you are sure to die."*
> *Genesis 2:15-17 (NLT)*

Of course they did that one thing and death became an eventuality. Sin separates us from God who gives life. However, the Bible tells us that human sin affects more than just humanity:

And to the man he said,
"Since you listened to your wife and ate from the tree
whose fruit I commanded you not to eat,
the ground is cursed because of you.
Genesis 3:17 (NLT)

Adam is affected by his own sin, he will die, but so too is the ground affected. Sin messes up everything. We see this theme carried on in the very next story:

"Why are you so angry?" the Lord asked Cain. "Why do you look so dejected? You will be accepted if you do what is right. But if you refuse to do what is right, then watch out! Sin is crouching at the door, eager to control you. But you must subdue it and be its master." One day Cain suggested to his brother, "Let's go out into the fields." And while they were in the field, Cain attacked his brother, Abel, and killed him. Genesis 4:6-8 (NLT)

Sin was "eager to control" Cain, but Abel, and Adam, and Eve, all suffered the consequences of Cain's sin. Before there was ever a death by the natural consequence of one's own sin, there was violent death as an unfortunate consequence of someone else's sin. Sin makes a mess of everything! It still does.

Consider a particularly cruel and selfish man whose attitudes and actions make life miserable for his family. He spreads the misery into his workplace like a bad virus. He then either gets fired, or his business runs down. The money runs out, and the house falls into ruin also. Sin messes everything up for everyone and everything, not just the person who sins.

In the Bible, Paul tells us that sin even makes a mess of creation:

> *For all creation is waiting eagerly for that future day when God will reveal who his children really are. Against its will, all creation was subjected to God's curse [as a result of the sin of humanity]. But with eager hope, the creation looks forward to the day when it will join God's children in glorious freedom from death and decay. Romans 8:19-21 (NLT)*

Creation is not waiting for God to wipe out humanity, so it can flourish on its own, but for God to rescue humanity, so it can flourish along with humanity. Brokenness in all creation is tied to human sinfulness. Restoration of creation is tied to the healing of humanity's sin problem.

So if the Christian Scriptures are accurate, then we should expect to live in a world where relationship with God is destroyed, where death is the expected and normal end for people, and where everything is messed up. This is exactly the world we live in! There is suffering because there is evil and sin, there is sin because there is freedom, there is freedom because God is love. It turns out that the world is exactly as we would expect if God is, and if God is love. Therefore the presence of evil and suffering lends support to the Bible's accuracy about the way things are.

But if God is love, would we not expect God to rescue us from evil and suffering? Indeed. The writings of the Bible tell us, from Genesis through to Revelation, that God is not content to leave humanity in a mess. God continued to work with humans. He did not just walk away.

God rescued a particular people from a messy situation, then gave them the law so that they would learn to not make a big mess of everything. For example, the Israelites were forbidden from practicing child-sacrifice. If they kept that law, there would be less evil and suffering in the world, for that practice was common in that time and place. The law was given to lead God's particular people out of evil so they could be an example to the other nations. However, they kept tripping on the way out.

All of this was part of a bigger plan for a bigger rescue. God came to us in Jesus and also provided his Spirit as part of that rescue. The two problems of sin are solved. First, we personally, and individually, experience reconciliation with God. Death, and separation from God, is no longer our final end. Second, when it comes to sin making a mess of everything, we are enabled to be part of Spirit-led solutions rather than part of sin-wrecked problems.

> *But the Holy Spirit produces this kind of fruit in our lives: love, joy, peace, patience, kindness, goodness, faithfulness, gentleness, and self-control. Galatians 5:22-23 (NLT)*

Just think of how much less suffering and evil there would be in the world if all lives were marked by these "fruit" of the Holy Spirit! As people participate in God's great rescue, our dark world should get brighter.

God's rescue is not limited to the possibility of individuals being reconciled to God and making less mess along the way. God will rescue all of creation:

> *Then I saw a new heaven and a new earth, for the old heaven and the old earth had disappeared. And the sea was also gone. And I saw the holy city, the new Jerusalem, coming down from God out of heaven like a bride beautifully dressed for her husband.*
>
> *I heard a loud shout from the throne, saying, "Look, God's home is now among his people! He will live with them, and they will be his people. God himself will be with them. He will wipe every tear from their eyes, and there will be no more death or sorrow or crying or pain. All these things are gone forever."*
> *And the one sitting on the throne said, "Look, I am making everything new!" And then he said to me, "Write this down, for what I tell you is trustworthy and true." And he also said, "It is finished! I am the Alpha and the Omega—the Beginning and the End. To all who are thirsty I will give freely from the springs of the water of life. All who are victorious will inherit all these blessings, and I will be their God, and they will be my children. Revelation 21:1-7 (NLT)*

Christianity provides a believable reason why evil and suffering exist in a world created by a loving God. There is suffering because there is sin, there is sin because there is freedom, there is freedom because God is love. Sin messes up everything. God knows, and since God is love, a Divine rescue is underway. The presence of evil and suffering in the world does not prove God does not exist nor does not care. It confirms what we learn from the Biblical writings. People sin, God is, and God is love.

A BELIEVABLE EXPLANATION OF THE BIBLE?

Does the existence and nature of the Bible point to the existence and nature of God? Some people just love the Bible. Some find reading it a head-scratching experience. Some hate it. Perhaps there might be some selective reading involved for any of the above. I suspect that many who love the Bible, and are never driven to question their faith because of what is says, stick to their favourite bits. Likewise, I suspect that those who question Christianity tend stick to their favourite tricky bits. We want to consider the Bible in its entirety as we ask whether it is a believable aspect of Christianity. Does the existence and nature of the Bible actually point to the reality of God?

Our expectations of the Bible play a big role in how we respond to it and whether we will find it compelling or not. People often have two expectations as they consider the Bible. Either it is written by God, or it is written by people, mainly men. Let us consider how these expectations pan out.

If the Bible was written by God, and if it was simply "downloaded" to us as if God sent us an email, then it is not what we would expect. It is convoluted. There are obviously so many authors writing at different times, under different circumstances, writing for different reasons, using different genres reflecting the kinds of writing humans do. It is not simply a "here are some messages from God with all humans, at all times, and in all situations in mind" kind of book. Indeed what we think of as one book is really many writings written and collected over a very long period of time. That much is obvious.

In addition, the Bible answers questions we are not asking today. Have you ever wondered who the great-great-grandson of Esau was? The Bible gives us the answer along with many other facts you are likely not interested in.

The Bible, however, does not answer some of the questions we are asking. What about the dinosaurs? Who did Cain marry? How do we ethically use all our advances in medicine? If the Bible is simply a direct message from God, would we not expect it to be a simple message that anticipates all the questions of humanity?

Therefore, **the Bible is not what we would expect it to be if it is simply a message written and sent by God.**

However, if the Bible is purely written out of the imagination of humans then likewise, it is not what we would expect. While there are some variances of thinking we should not gloss over, overall there is an amazing consistency in the presentation of God, the nature of humanity, the human dilemma, and the relationship between God and humanity. Despite the number of writings, the differing authors from different centuries living under different conditions, there is an incredible sense of unity in the Bible. There is also an incredible storyline that spans the many, many, many generations that lived while the writings were being written. Each generation would have had trouble making up its own part in that overall story.

Therefore **the Bible is not what we would expect it to be if it is simply a product of the human mind.**

So what is the Bible, then, if the Bible is not what we would expect if God simply sent us a direct message, or if we made God and the Bible up on our own?

The writings we find in the Bible are the kinds of writings we would expect if God created humanity, then humanity rebelled, then God chose and called a specific people for the working out of His purposes, made covenant promises with them, rescued them from Egypt, gave them the law at Sinai, established covenant promises and consequences consistent with society at that time, brought them into a promised land where the people kept breaking the covenant, then appointed leaders and prophets to get them back on track while continuing to reveal more of His purposes, then He came to us as a man, teaching, working miracles, was killed, then rose from the dead, appeared to many, gave the Holy Spirit, then the many people who saw him alive went about as witnesses telling others what they knew to be true, while God gave the Holy Spirit to people who were not from His specifically chosen people so they could be in relationship with Him also, while groups of believers gathered together in assemblies which sometimes needed instructions which was given through letters written by Paul and others, while the stories about, and teachings of, Jesus, were committed to writing by four men in what came to be known as the Gospels. **If all these things happened and more, then the Bible is exactly the collection of writings we would expect.**

The opposite is true. If these things did not happen, then why do the writings that make up the Bible exist, why do they take the shape they do, and why do they say the things they do?

The writings that make up the Bible are records of the ongoing relationship between God and humanity throughout many centuries in history until God finally revealed Himself most fully through Jesus:

> *Long ago God spoke many times and in many ways to our ancestors through the prophets. And now in these final days, he has spoken to us through his Son. God promised everything to the Son as an inheritance, and through the Son he created the universe. The Son radiates God's own glory and expresses the very character of God, and he sustains everything by the mighty power of his command. When he had cleansed us from our sins, he sat down in the place of honor at the right hand of the majestic God in heaven.*
> Hebrews 1:1-3 (NLT)

So are these writings from God therefore to be considered "The Word of God," or are they simply what humans wrote? They are both. Consider what Paul says of the sacred writings, what we now call "The Bible,"

> *But as for you, continue in what you have learned and have become convinced of, because you know those from whom you learned it, and how from infancy you have known the Holy Scriptures, which are able to make you wise for salvation through faith in Christ Jesus. All Scripture is God-breathed and is useful for teaching, rebuking, correcting and training in righteousness, so that the servant of God may be thoroughly equipped for every good work. 2 Timothy 3:14-17 (NIV emphasis added)*

The writings that make up the Bible are "God breathed." That means they are not simply written by God and downloaded to us, nor are they simply written by men without God's involvement. Both God and humans are involved. They absolutely passed through the minds of people, they were absolutely penned by people and according to their understanding, but they absolutely have God's blessing as expressing what we need to know. God would not have a long, long history of relationship with humanity, culminating with His very coming to us to enable relationship with Him, without providing for an accurate representation to be written and collected for future generations. So the writings of the Bible are "God breathed," which means they are neither "God written," nor "human invented." Both God and humans are involved.

When the writings of the Bible seem to be from another time and place, we are not surprised. They were written by people in another time and place who also held different ways of looking at things. When the writings of the Bible seem timeless we are not surprised. The creator of time, who still relates to us in our time, was involved!

Since this is the nature of the Bible, we want to check our expectations. The Bible is described by Paul as being "able to make you wise for salvation through faith in Christ Jesus," and useful for "training in righteousness." This means it is not a handbook to answer every question and satisfy our curiosity. Neither is it an idol to be worshipped. It does help us know the Divine, whom we do worship. Knowing about reconciliation in Jesus is infinitely better than knowing about the dinosaurs, or where Cain found a wife!

The Bible is not what we would expect if God simply sent us a direct message, nor if we simply made it all up. However, it is what we would expect if God has had a long relationship with us, interacting with us throughout history, and wants to be known. The Bible itself, in all its convoluted mess, in all its wonderful consistency and amazing storyline, is believable evidence that God exists and that God loves us.

A BELIEVABLE EXPLANATION OF JESUS?

Who is Jesus and why should we care? Some suggest that we should think about Jesus apart from any religious ideas, that is, without asking the "God question." Let us do so for a moment. Before we ask whether God exists, or, if Jesus has anything to do with said God, what can we say about Jesus? Here are some things:

Jesus was a man of compelling activity. He went about doing good. Life-changing miracles are ascribed to him, but even if your worldview is not open to miracles, you can at least say that the earliest witnesses knew Jesus to be a man of good works done for the sake of many people.

Jesus was a man of compelling teaching. He is described as teaching "with authority" and "not like the teachers of the law"[27]. He was not formally educated, yet was recognised as having better teaching than the educated and sophisticated teachers.

---

[27] see Mark 1:22.

Jesus was a man of compelling ethics. His vision for how we should treat one another was focused on love long before the Beatles sang "all you need is love." In contrast to the religious leaders of the day, Jesus pointed out that divine rules existed for the sake of humans, rather than humans existing for the sake of the rules[28].

Jesus had a compelling presence. He was known as a friend to sinners[29]. Despite his profound teaching and capability, things which can often make people inaccessible to others, he was a man of the people. People longed for and enjoyed his presence.

Jesus issued a compelling challenge whenever necessary. Whether telling the woman caught in adultery to "go and sin no more"[30] or, as happened far more often, challenging the religious leaders, the status quo had no chance in the presence of Jesus.

Jesus issued a compelling life-changing and world-changing call. It was expected, even hoped for, that Jesus would call people to pick up a sword and fight the Romans. Instead Jesus called people to pick up a cross and follow[31]. His call was to the way of understanding, love, grace, and forgiveness.

[28] see, for example, Mark 2:27.

[29] see Matthew 11:16-19.

[30] see John 8:11.

[31] see Matthew 16:24-26.

Jesus had, and continues to have, a compelling impact.
Even if you do not believe in God, or that Jesus is God, you cannot deny that Jesus has had a huge positive impact in the lives of individuals, in entire societies, and indeed upon the world. Yes, Christians at times have had, and continue to have, a negative impact, but the impact of Jesus has been profoundly positive and enduring.

We could describe Jesus as the most compelling person in the history of the world. We have not even considered the "God question" yet. Let us now do so.

In Mark 8:27-30 Jesus asked the disciples "Who do people say that I am?", followed with "who do you say that I am?". This is perhaps the most important question ever asked. Peter answers "You are the Messiah," which shows that Peter was beginning to recognise that Jesus was from God in some special way.

We can also ask "who does Jesus say he is?". Consider these words from Jesus;

> *"I am the living bread that came down from heaven" John 6:51*
> *"I am the light of the world" John 8:12*
> *"You are from below, I am from above; you are of this world, I am not of this world." John 8:23*
> *"If God were your Father, you would love me, for I came from God and now I am here. I did not come on my own, but he sent me." John 8:42*

"Very truly, I tell you, before Abraham was, I am." John 8:58

"I am the good shepherd. The good shepherd lays down his life for the sheep." John 10:11

"I am the resurrection and the life. Those who believe in me, even though they die, will live," John 11:25

"I am the way, and the truth, and the life. No one comes to the Father except through me. If you know me, you will know my Father also. From now on you do know him and have seen him." John 14:6-7

In case there is any doubt that Jesus had a very high opinion of himself:

For this reason the Jews were seeking all the more to kill him, because he was not only breaking the sabbath, but was also calling God his own Father, thereby making himself equal to God. John 5:18

Let us also consider that this high view of Jesus is consistent with all the New Testament witnesses. All the New Testament writers affirm, or are in tune with the belief that, Jesus is God the Son. Take for example the opening of the Gospel of Mark, which is the most "down to earth" of the four Gospels;

The beginning of the good news of Jesus Christ, the Son of God.
As it is written in the prophet Isaiah,

"See, I am sending my messenger ahead of you,
who will prepare your way;
the voice of one crying out in the wilderness:
'Prepare the way of the Lord,
make his paths straight,' " Mark 1:1-3

This reference to Old Testament prophecy in Mark is not in mere anticipation of a Messiah, a man anointed by God to rescue the people from oppressors. That is not what the prophecy in Isaiah is about. This is anticipation of God Himself arriving. The Gospel of Mark, while being about Jesus, is about God coming to us. These are one and the same thing.

Jesus taught that he was from God, that He came from God in a special way which could not be said of anyone else. But do we believe him? If a person we considered evil, like Stalin, said the kind of things about himself that Jesus said about himself, would we believe him? Given his life, you'd say "Nope!". Likewise, if you said the kinds of things about yourself that Jesus said about himself, would anyone believe you? Again, "Nope!". But when Jesus says it, with his compelling activity, teaching, ethics, presence, challenge, call, and impact, plus the eyewitness testimony of people saying, "he was dead but lives!", well, that is different.

Consider also, if God were to come to us as one of us, if He were to become incarnate, especially the kind of promise-making-and-keeping God we find in the Old Testament, what would He be like? We would expect Him to have compelling activity, teaching, ethics, presence, challenge, call, and impact. Because He is love, we would expect a rescue. Because He is powerful we would expect victory over death. Jesus fits our expectation of what God should look like!

Who Jesus was, who people experienced him to be, adds weight to who he said he is. Of course Jesus is the most compelling person in history. We would expect that from someone who is "God with us"[32], "Lord"[33], and the "Lamb who takes away the sin of the world"[34]. He is the great God and love solution to the great human problem of hatred and death.

Jesus is the most compelling person in the history of the world, even without the God question. Add in the God question and the God answer to the human problem, and Jesus is even more compelling! Jesus is evidence that God is, and that God is love. Being a compelling man, Jesus is yet more evidence that Christianity is believable.

---

[32] see Matthew 1:23

[33] see Romans 10:9

[34] see John 1:29

A BELIEVABLE RESURRECTION?

Can we really believe that Jesus rose from the dead? If someone told you they had a friend who spontaneously rose from the dead three days after dying, would you believe them? Probably not, and that is good, for doubt and scepticism are important tools in helping us avoid deception and discover truth. If we would not believe a report about a friend being raised in three days, then why believe it with regards to Jesus?

First off, let us remember the nature of the Bible. It does not present itself as a simple system of beliefs or ethics, or a series of philosophical ideas, but instead as a series of sometimes convoluted history lessons and how what happened in history affected people's beliefs and ideas. For the person of faith it is the history of God's interactions with humanity. For the unbeliever, the historical aspect is still important. These writings appeared in history for some reason. When we consider the writings of the New Testament, even a very sceptical person will want to consider what happened that;

1. caused the body of Jesus to not be in the tomb in which he was laid, nor ever be produced as evidence when certain people clearly wanted the "rumours" of a resurrection to be squashed.

2. caused many people to go around saying that they saw Jesus risen from the dead and be willing to die for that testimony.

3. caused naysayers like James, and especially Paul, to change their tune despite a very devout devotion to Judaism. Paul went from persecuting Christians for their supposed blasphemy to being one. Why?

4. caused theology to develop within the New Testament which has some surprising and unexpected twists. It was expected that God would rescue His people. It was expected that God would send a messiah. It was expected that there would be a resurrection of all people at the end of the age. It was not expected that God would rescue people through himself becoming a suffering messiah who would be executed then rise from the dead, quite apart from a resurrection of everyone else.

What happened to cause these things?

Were the disciples hallucinating? Perhaps the disciples were so distraught that they all just thought they saw Jesus? The possibility of mass hallucinations is fraught with problems from the get-go, plus the hallucinations theory does not explain the new boldness of the disciples, the empty tomb, the turn-arounds in Paul and James, nor the surprising new twists in theology.

Did the disciples steal the body of Jesus, then make up the story of the resurrection? This would explain the empty tomb, but would not explain why the disciples were not only willing to die for their testimony, but able. No one broke down and shared a different story! It also does not explain the change in Paul or James. Nor is it likely they would have made up a story and developed a theology which ensured persecution from both Jewish and Roman antagonists alike.

Perhaps Jesus did not really die? However, the Romans were recognised as being very capable at putting people to death. Also, why the change in Paul and James, neither of whom were disciples before the events of Easter? A battered and bruised Jesus would hardly be convincing. Why the interesting and unusual new twists in theological reflection?

If you are open to the possibility of a miracle happening, an actual resurrection of Jesus is the simplest explanation that accounts for all the evidence. The resurrection explains everything; why the tomb was empty and a body was never produced, why the disciples were willing to die for their testimony of seeing Jesus alive and boldly stuck to the story, why sceptics like James and Paul changed their tune, and why theology developed in an unexpected way.

If you are open to the possibility of a miracle. There lies the problem for many people. However, we have already looked at compelling reasons to believe in a creator God, a miracle working God. The cosmos points to the reality of God. Our minds point to the reality of God, as does the existence of evil, the fact of morality, and the existence and nature of the Bible. Reasonable people can be open to the existence of a creator God, and therefore be open to the miraculous. If you are open to the possibility of a miracle, the resurrection of Jesus is the best explanation of all the facts.

Consider also, that the resurrection of Jesus was not a random occurrence that came out of the blue. Rather this is an event in history which fits the compelling nature of Jesus. What he did, what he taught, how he related to people, it was all extraordinary. His resurrection may be surprising, indeed extraordinary, but it makes sense given how extraordinary Jesus was known to be.

The resurrection is also an event in history which fits what the Old Testament was pointing to all along. The death and resurrection of Jesus confirms what we should expect to be true about God, that God is perfect in justice and in love. While a story of spontaneous resurrection would normally be considered nonsense, the resurrection of Jesus happened in a context in which it makes sense.

In considering the context of the resurrection of Jesus, we can also consider the purpose. If Jesus rose from the dead, we also can look forward to resurrection to eternal life. The resurrection is evidence that Jesus is Lord and that God has done something about our death problem. The resurrection of Jesus is not some random event devoid of meaning, but one which fulfills a purpose.

Last, but not least, the resurrection of Jesus makes sense of the experience many of us have of Jesus making a difference in our lives!

Can we, as intelligent, thinking, people, really believe that Jesus rose from the dead? Yes, not only can we, there are reasons to do so. The events of Easter point to the reality of the God we discover in the Bible. The events of Easter as recorded in the writings of the Bible point to the reality of God's love.

CONCLUSION

But in your hearts revere Christ as Lord. Always be prepared to give an answer to everyone who asks you to give the reason for the hope that you have. But do this with gentleness and respect... 1 Peter 3:15 (NIV)

While I was raised in a Christian home, that is not the reason why I am a Christian. Indeed over the years there have been reasons that I have wanted to turn my back on Christianity. However, there are reasons why I continue to be a follower of Jesus. Though I myself have sometimes expressed Christianity in ugly ways, I have discovered that a Jesus centred faith is beautiful. Though I have a sceptical mind and still have unanswered questions, I have learned that a Jesus focused faith is believable. That a Jesus focused faith is both beautiful and believable is the reason for my hope.

Perhaps you still have questions. I do. But do we need all the answers? I have long thought of faith as being like a jigsaw puzzle. Some people start with the most difficult questions and give up on Jesus and Christianity before there is any chance of seeing any picture in the puzzle. But with a little effort, and the leaving aside of the most difficult questions for a time, the puzzle pieces come together in such a way that a picture begins to form. It is a beautiful picture. So beautiful, in fact, that many of us cannot help but keep working on it despite the fact we don't think we will ever finish it.

As with a jigsaw puzzle, sometimes there are tricky pieces that we cannot yet place. Sometimes it feels like we are forcing certain pieces together to get them to fit, and we are uncomfortable with that. Sometimes we need to take pieces out that we thought fit, and fit them in somewhere else. This is all a normal part of growing and maturing in our understanding and depth of faith. But it is beautiful picture, and well worth the effort. It is a picture of love, of God's love in Jesus.

Let us finish back at the photo on the cover. My prayer is that you find a Jesus focused faith to be beautiful and believable and that you take the plunge if you have not already. If you do not, then I pray that you keep searching, keeping Jesus in mind as you do. Maybe someday...

FOR FURTHER READING

Boa, Ken. 20 Compelling Evidences That God Exists: Discover Why Believing in God Makes So Much Sense. David C. Cook, 2013. (Kindle)

Boyd, Gregory A. and Edward K. Boyd. Letters from a Skeptic: A Son Wrestles with His Father's Questions about Christianity. David C. Cook, 2010. (Kindle)

Craig, William Lane. On Guard: Defending Your Faith with Reason and Precision. David C. Cook. 2010.

Craig, Willam Lane. Reasonable Faith: Christian Truth and Apologetics. Crossway, 2008.

D'Souza Dinesh. Godforsaken: Bad Things Happen. Is there a God who cares? Yes. He"s proof. Tyndale House, 2012. (Kindle)

Edwards, Michael. Gravity True For You But Not For Me: Evidence for God's Existence and Identity. Kindle Ebooks.

Geisel, Norman L. Reasons for Belief: Easy-to-Understand Answers to 10 Essential Questions. Bethany House, 2013. (Kindle)

Groothius, David. Christian Apologetics: A Comprehensive Case for Biblical Faith. Inter Varsity Press, 2011. (Kindle)

Hitchens, Peter. The Rage Against God. How Atheism Led Me to Faith. Zondervan, 2010. (Kobo)

Koukl, Gregory. Tactics. a game plan for discussing your Christian convictions. Zondervan, 2009.

Lennox, John C. Seven Days That Divide the World. Zondervan, 2011.

Lewis, C.S. Mere Christianity. (Kindle)

McDowell, Josh. Did the Resurrection Happen . . .Really?: A Dialogue on Life, Death, and Hope (The Coffee House Chronicles Book 3). Moody, 2011 (Kindle)

McDowell, Josh. Is the Bible True . . .Really?: A Dialogue on Skepticism, Evidence, and Truth (The Coffee House Chronicles Book 1). Moody, 2011 (Kindle)

Quereshi, Nabeel A. Seeking Allah, Finding Jesus. Zondervan, 2014 (Apple Books)

Ross, Hugh. The Creator and the Cosmos: How the Latest Scientific Discoveries Reveal God. Reasons to Believe, 2018 (Kindle Edition)

Schmidt, Alvin J. How Christianity Changed the World. Zondervan, 2009. (Kindle)

Spiegel, James. The Making of an Atheist: How Immorality Leads to Unbelief. Moody, 2010. (Kindle)

Stark, Rodney. God's Battalions: The Case for the Crusades. HarperCollins, 2009. (Apple Books)

Strobel, Lee. The Case for a Creator. A Journalist Investigates Scientific Evidence That Points Toward God. Zondervan, 2005.

Strobel, Lee. The Case for Christ. A Journalist's Personal Investigation of the Evidence for Jesus. Zondervan. 1998.

Strobel, Lee. The Case for Faith. A Journalist Investigates the Toughest Objections to Christianity. Zondervan, 1999.

Wallace, J Warner. Cold-Case Christianity. A Homicide Detective Investigate the Claims of the Gospels. David C Cook. 2012

Wallace, J Warner. God's Crime Scene:A Cold-Case Detective Examines the Evidence for a Divinely Created Universe. David C Cook. 2015. (Apple Books)

Wright, N.T. Jesus and the Victory of God. SPCK, 1996.

Wright, N.T. The New Testament and the People of God. SPCK, 1992.

Wright, N.T. The Resurrection of the Son of God. SPCK, 2003.

ABOUT THE AUTHOR

Clarke was born in Northern Ireland but lived in Scotland until age six when his family moved to Canada. Clarke studied at Trent University, majoring in English Literature and Classical Studies, and McMaster Divinity College where he earned a Masters of Divinity in 1997. Clarke has been pastoring ever since and now serves at Calvary Baptist in Cobourg, Ontario.

Sandra and Clarke were married in 1999 and they have three sons. They now live in Colborne and enjoy trail running and kayaking together. Clarke also enjoys motorcycling, playing bass in a country rock band, and reading the Bible in Greek and Hebrew. Sandra does not, but does enjoy quilting.

Clarke's passion is to help people walk with Jesus in faith, hope, and love.